MINISTRY &
THEOLOGY

MINISTRY&
THEOLOGY

Studies for the Church and Its Leaders

John Christopher Thomas

PATHWAY
CLEVELAND, TENNESSEE 37311

Library of Congress
Catalog Card Number: 95-071828

ISBN: 871486008

Copyright © 1996 by Pathway Press

Cleveland, Tennessee 37311

Printed in the United States of America

As a token of my affection
I dedicate this book to my
mothers and fathers
sisters and brothers
daughters and sons
in the
Woodward Avenue Church of God.

CONTENTS

PREFACE

For more than a decade now it has been my honor and privilege to serve the church as a teacher at the Church of God School of Theology and as an associate pastor at the Woodward Avenue Church of God in Athens, Tennessee. In addition to the usual ministerial involvement that each of these placements entails, I have known the affirmation of having the church request that I write for it on several occasions.

This book is a collection of essays I have produced over the past several years. Although of varying lengths and written for differing occasions, they all have in common the fact that they were solicited by the church and, therefore, represent reflection on relevant issues of ministry and theology facing the church and its leaders. Chapters 1 and 2 were written for the *Church of God Evangel*; chapters 3 and 5, for *The Pentecostal Minister*; chapter 4, for *On Guard*; chapters 6 and 9, for the Church of God School of Theology's annual Seminar on Ministry; chapters 7, 10, and 11, for the denomination's annual conference for state and general leadership; chapter 12, for the Women in Ministry Conference; and chapter 8, at the request of the general overseer of the Church of God.

By offering these studies for publication in this form, I desire to make them available to a wider audience within the church. May the Lord use them as He desires.

ACKNOWLEDGMENTS

Without the aid and support of a number of people, the publication of this book would not have been possible. First, I would like to express my appreciation to Kenneth T. Harvell, Homer G. Rhea, and Harold Medford of Pathway Press for accepting this volume for publication. Their willingness to take a risk on the work of a young scholar is both encouraging and visionary.

Special thanks are also due my colleagues and students (past and present) at the Church of God School of Theology. Through their commitment to constructive Pentecostal theology and their genuine interest in me and my work, they have served as a constant source of spiritual support and intellectual stimulation over the years. Specifically, Rick D. Moore, Cheryl Bridges Johns, and Steven J. Land have given of their time and energies to think through a variety of issues with me and have made an enormous impact on my life and thought. One of my former graduate assistants, Jerry Ingram, not only assisted me in most every aspect of my work but also facilitated this publication by placing the bulk of this work on computer disk.

The sacrifices of my wife, Barbara, and my daughters, Paige and Lori, have been enormous for this and many other writing projects. Their love, nurture, and care make most every task pleasurable and every day meaningful. They are, without doubt, my greatest joy; their dedication to and maturation in the Lord, my greatest blessing.

Finally, I wish to express my love and heartfelt thanks to the Woodward Avenue Church of God in Athens, Tennessee. I have been a part of this body of believers since 1973. This remarkable community of faith has continually surprised me by its loving commitment to our Lord, its acceptance of and identification with the poor and oppressed, and its unswerving loyalty to the mission to which God has called it. The sensitive spiritual leadership of my pastors and parents, Wayne and Betty Fritts, is extraordinarily refreshing in this day of manipulation and superficiality. Much of what I know of the church and its ministry I have learned from this congregation and these servants of the Lord, and I am happy to acknowledge here my indebtedness to them.

As a token of my affection, I dedicate this book to my mothers and fathers, sisters and brothers, sons and daughters of the Woodward Avenue Church of God.

THE WORD
AND THE SPIRIT

The Bible is the Christian's most treasured book. Next to Jesus, it is regarded as the fullest revelation of God. In this light, many Christians believe that the Bible was produced through a divine initiative. Throughout the centuries the church has confessed that the Bible is an inspired document.

Pentecostals and the Inspiration of Scripture

From the beginning of the movement, Pentecostals generally, and the Church of God in particular, have held an extremely high view of Scripture. One reason for their belief that Scripture is divinely inspired is that a number of Pentecostals came into the movement from fundamentalist backgrounds and simply brought their view of inspiration with them. But perhaps another powerful contributing factor for this belief concerned the Pentecostals' sudden awareness of the immediate and direct ministry of the Holy Spirit through Spirit baptism, spiritual gifts, and other manifestations. If, as Pentecostals had come to learn, the Holy Spirit could manifest Himself in such powerful ways in the lives of ordinary men and women, then it was easy to believe that He could inspire human beings to produce the Bible.

Yet despite their fervent belief in the inspiration of the Scriptures, many Pentecostal groups made simple statements about inspiration, leaving unsaid many of the things their non-Pentecostal counterparts would have stated. For example, the earliest official Church of God statement about Scripture (*Evangel*, August 15, 1910) said, "The Church of God stands for the whole Bible rightly divided. The New Testament is the only rule for government and discipline." This brief statement, which was adopted in the General Assembly of 1911, proved adequate for nearly 40 years. When the church adopted a more detailed statement in the Declaration of Faith, it contained a more expansive statement on inspiration, similar to that of the National Association of Evangelicals. At the 1948 General Assembly, the following article was adopted: "We believe in the verbal inspiration of the Bible."

Such a history should not be taken to suggest that Pentecostals did not always believe wholeheartedly in the inspiration of Scripture, but that Pentecostals had their own concerns alongside the debates that were mostly going on elsewhere within the Evangelical community.

The Current Debate

At the present time, a number of churches are experiencing division over the issue of the inspiration of the Bible. Denominations, missionary boards, publishing houses, and educational institutions are being fought over by opposing factions. As emotional, and sometimes heated, arguments are being made by both sides, it is easy to be drawn into the fray.

Before joining ranks with combatants who may not represent Pentecostal life and thought, however, Pentecostals need to clarify certain issues about the nature and purpose of inspiration. Insofar as inspiration concerns the work of the Spirit, it is just possible that Pentecostals have something distinctive to say. The rest of this chapter focuses on these issues.

What Does "Inspiration" Mean?

The only place the word *inspiration* occurs in Scripture with reference to "inspired documents" is 2 Timothy 3:16. Here it is stated that all Scripture is profitable for teaching, rebuking, correcting, and training in righteousness because it is inspired. The Greek word translated "inspiration" is actually a compound term which combines roots from the words *God* and *spirit/breathe* (θεόπνευστος). Most Bible scholars have concluded that the word *inspiration* literally means "breathed into by God."

Another passage which bears on the issue of inspiration is found in 2 Peter 1:20, 21. In this passage, the biblical writer states that the Old Testament prophecies were not the result of human imagination but the result of the Holy Spirit's activity. Here the prophets are likened to sailors who have raised the sails of their ships, and the Holy Spirit to the wind which carries them along in the direction of His choosing.

Both of these texts make clear that the Scriptures are of divine origin and that God himself was active in their composition, breathing into them, carrying them along. These verses demonstrate that Scripture cannot be properly appreciated apart from divine inspiration. However, neither of these passages describes the precise way in which these writers were inspired. Consequently, another question must be raised.

How Does Inspiration Work?

A proper definition of inspiration must be sensitive to the various ways in which individuals were inspired to write the documents that make up the Bible. Surprisingly enough, God did not choose to inspire everyone in an identical fashion. That is not to say that some portions of Scripture are more inspired than others, but rather to underscore the fact that God inspired the biblical writers in a variety of ways (Hebrews 1:1). Several examples illustrate this point.

Some portions of Scripture are explicitly identified as coming from God's own hand (Deuteronomy 4:13; 10:1-5). A number of other passages began as divinely inspired prophetic utterances, where for all practical purposes the spokesperson is merely God's mouthpiece. This conclusion is evidenced by the fact that many times God's speech is uttered in the first person.

Several books were written by means of a secretary, who put into writing the words of another. Paul, who made use of such help (Romans 16:22), sometimes wrote portions of his letters in his own hand. In such cases he usually emphasized this point (1 Corinthians 16:21; Colossians 4:18; 2 Thessalonians 3:17).

Baruch, Jeremiah's secretary, not only recorded the words which Jeremiah dictated (Jeremiah 36:32) but seems to have also played an active role in the composition of the book itself, since many passages record episodes in the life of Jeremiah from the perspective of an onlooker.

While some books were based, at least in part, on eyewitness testimony (John 21:24), others are clearly based upon research (Luke 1:3). In fact, large portions of the Old Testament seem to be the work of anonymous writers who, under the inspiration of the Spirit, searched through many sources in the production of their own work (1 Kings 11:41; 14:29; 15:31). Some portions of the Proverbs are drawn from the work of figures who are apparently non-Israelite (cf. Proverbs 30:1; 31:1).

What Do Inspired Documents Look Like?

Despite the fact that Scripture is divinely inspired, the books that make up the Bible sounds amazingly like other literature. Within the Bible one can find law, history, poetry, songs, letters, and sermons. In fact, most kinds of biblical literature find a parallel in noncanonical writings, except perhaps for the Gospels, which seem to be an unparalleled literary form. Yet, rather than denying these similarities, biblical writers are known to acknowledge them and make comparisons with them (see 1 Kings 4:29-34).

Such similarities serve to underscore the fact that God has chosen to reveal Himself through a book which has both a divine side and a human side. Although the Holy Spirit breathed into the human writers when He moved upon them, He did not obliterate their personalities but used their abilities, vocabularies, writing styles, and literary forms to reveal and record His Word. There may be a temptation to disregard the human side of Scripture in order to protect its divine nature. However, following such an impulse can result in an unhealthy imbalance which obscures the nature and richness of God's written revelation, just as disregarding the human nature of Jesus distorts the character and essence of His incarnation.

The Word, the Spirit, and the Church

The Bible of the early church was the Old Testament. But as time passed, a number of Christian documents began to circulate, each claiming to be authoritative to one degree or another. As a result, the church faced the dilemma of determining which documents were worthy of special attention and which documents were not.

It is sometimes stated that particular church councils decided upon which books were to make up the New Testament. But such explanations are much too simplistic. In point of fact, these later church councils seem to have placed their approval on the documents that had already come to be recognized by the church at large as being inspired by the Holy Spirit. Their role was less to determine the canon of Scripture than simply to recognize what was already operative as canon throughout the church.

In other words, it appears that through the use of Scripture in its life and worship, the early church was able to discern and respond to those documents which were, in fact, inspired. This was accomplished because the Holy Spirit placed His unmistakable imprint upon the New Testament documents. The church was in a position to recognize these inspired texts because it was accustomed to the ministry of the Holy Spirit through Spirit baptism, the bestowal of spiritual gifts, and other spiritual manifestations even before there was a New Testament. As a result, the 66 books of the Bible are the product of the providential work of God.

The dynamic interplay between the Word, the Spirit, and the church did not cease when the Bible was complete. It must be maintained in order for the church to continue its ministry in this world.

The Sum of the Matter

What implications concerning the inspiration of the Scripture may be drawn for Pentecostals from this short study?

1. While a high view of Scripture is a normal part of orthodox Christianity, it is no guarantee of doctrinal integrity. Many odd and heretical views have come from individuals espousing an extremely high view of Scripture.

2. Unnecessary controversies and fights about a specific definition of inspiration may produce individuals and groups who are so preoccupied with the letter of Scripture that they miss what the Spirit desires to tell the church through the Word of God.

3. There is a tendency among some of the radical proponents of inspiration to reduce the role of the Holy Spirit to the pages of Scripture itself—in effect, placing God in a box. Pentecostals must continue to insist that the ministry of the Holy Spirit cannot be reduced to His role in the inspiration of Scripture.

4. There is a danger that so much attention may be focused on a particular view of inspiration that the life

of the church becomes stunted and the mission of the church rendered ineffective.

5. For Pentecostals, inspiration of Scripture must never become an end in itself, but must remain the starting point. It is not enough to believe that the Scriptures are inspired; one must live in a way that testifies that those Scriptures are inspired.

6. The divinely inspired Word of God is the norm by which teaching, doctrine, works of the Spirit, and ministerial practices are to be evaluated and judged. Therefore, a high view of Scripture is a necessity.

As debates about Scripture continue, it is important for Pentecostals to maintain their focus on the mission that lies before the church. While others argue about Scripture, Pentecostals should continue to put Scripture into practice. The night is far spent, and the Lord's appearing is near (Romans 13:12).

THE ESSENCE OF WORSHIP

The mention of worship usually produces thoughts of singing, praying, giving, and preaching. While these are some of the elements used in the worship of God, they do not in themselves constitute worship. It is important to study the elements of worship, for this results in a better understanding of their appropriate use. However, an even more important and basic study concerns the very essence of worship. What does it mean to worship?

The English word *worship* actually means "worthship." It conveys the idea of ascribing worth to someone or something. This automatically centers attention on God as the object of our worship instead of on self. Rather than thinking in terms of "blessings," focus is directed to the worthiness of God.

One of the fundamentals in identifying the essence of worship is understanding the relationship between God and humankind. This involves the recognition of who God is. The following three areas of God's activity tell a great deal about His identity.

God Is Creator

The Scriptures are full of information about this role of God. Everything owes its existence to Him. The crowning glory of creation is the human being, male and female. This creature was the last to be created and bears the special imprint of the Creator's image. The purpose of the entire creation, and the human being in particular, is to bring glory to God. Much of the glory lies in the uniqueness of the creation. No other god is able to create or even give advice (Isaiah 40; Job 38).

God Is Redeemer

More than anything else, the Bible is a book about redemption. It can be called a history of salvation. From His dealings with Adam and Eve to the crucifixion and resurrection of Jesus, God demonstrated His desire to redeem men and women from the power of sin. The only possible way in which humanity can be liberated from sin is through the miraculous Incarnation, when "the Word became flesh." The Old Testament believers looked forward to the Messiah and were justified in advance, while the New Testament believers are able to look back on what has been accomplished. Abraham is the example of how God deals with human beings. Because he believed, Abraham was counted righteous. Salvation comes no other way.

God Is Sustainer

Through His awesome abilities the universe continues to exist. The world will come to an end when *He* says it will. His sustaining work is exhibited in the life of the believer as well. To be justified in God's sight is a wonderful thing, but without the regenerating power of the Holy Spirit there could be no chance of living a holy life. By the new birth the individual is a new creature. God sustains this new life through His love and care. He enables the believer to live the life he/she is intended to live.

It is a short step from here to the essence of worship. Realizing who God is calls forth a certain response from the believer. To know that one is utterly dependent produces a grateful heart of humility. How is it that God—the Creator, the Redeemer, and the Sustainer—is interested in the creature (Psalm 8:4)? The essence of worship is not only knowing who God is, but it is also knowing who we are. Consequently, worship is responding to God as Creator, Redeemer, and Sustainer. This is not to be confined to what traditionally is called worship but is to be evident in attitudes and lifestyles as well.

Everything done should reflect on God's worthship. As creatures, lives must exhibit a striving for the potentials that are inbred into the human. As redeemed, humankind must demonstrate in every aspect of existence the kind of life intended by God for His creation. As the sustained, men and women must show an attitude of humility and expectancy toward the gracious Father.

The essence of worship is responding to the absolute worthship of God with lives that exhibit God's intentions for humanity. For in all these things God is glorified.

CHAPTER 3

THE KINGDOM OF GOD AND THE NEW TESTAMENT

The meaning of the kingdom of God is a significant and widely debated topic among contemporary believers. Unfortunately, a great deal of confusion surrounds the discussion. This situation is due in part to the complex nature of the biblical material on the subject. Also, inaccurate biblical interpretation often compounds the issue.

Although the present state of affairs is not always desirable, it is often in such situations that the church is able to reexamine the Scripture and come to a more precise understanding of a biblical doctrine or teaching. It is reasonable to assume that as the church grapples with the biblical understanding of the kingdom of God, a more balanced interpretation will emerge.

Terminology and Definition

Identifying and defining the terminology Scripture uses to designate the phenomenon of the Kingdom is essential for this study. Primarily in the New Testament two terms are used for the Kingdom: *the kingdom of God* and *the kingdom of heaven.* The first term occurs more frequently than the second. Matthew, however, exhibits an obvious preference for *kingdom of heaven.* Some suggest that Matthew intended to make a distinction between the kingdom of heaven and kingdom of God, for in addition to his usual use of *kingdom of heaven,* the Book of Matthew contains four references to *kingdom of God.* Such a suggestion lacks biblical support, however. This observation may be demonstrated by comparing parallel passages in Matthew, Mark, and Luke (Matthew 13:11; Mark 4:11; Luke 8:10; Matthew 13:31, 33; Mark 4:30; Luke 13:18, 20; Matthew 19:14; Mark 10:15; Luke 18:17; Matthew 19:23; Mark 10:23, 25; Luke 18:24-26). In each case Matthew used *kingdom of heaven,* while Mark and Luke used *kingdom of God.* Consequently, both terms refer to the same phenomenon.

What accounts for Matthew's distinctive terminology? On the one hand, it appears that he substituted *heaven* for *God* for the sake of Jewish Christians in the church, who were reluctant to pronounce the divine name. On the other hand, when Matthew used *kingdom of God* instead of *kingdom of heaven* (12:28; 19:24; 21:31, 43), it must be for the sake of emphasis.[1]

The meaning of the kingdom of God has more to do with the reign or rule of God than the realm of the

---

[1]For a more comprehensive discussion of this issue see my article "The Kingdom of God in the Gospel according to Matthew," *New Testament Studies,* Vol. 39 (1993), pp. 136-146.

Kingdom. In other words, the Kingdom denotes the authority and sovereignty of God to reign, not necessarily the geographical domain of the King.

The Kingdom of God and the Old Testament

In the Old Testament there is evidence of the kingdom of God. In fact, the idea of God as King is at the very heart of Israelite religion. In the Exodus, Yahweh replaced Pharaoh as King of the Israelites (Exodus 15:18), and the Sinai covenant cast the faith of Israel in a treaty form which presents the terms by which a king governs his servants.

Many other Old Testament texts identify Yahweh as King and/or proclaim His kingdom (1 Chronicles 29:11; Psalms 22:27, 28; 103:19; 145:11-13; Isaiah 43:15; Daniel 4:3). As Creator, He is King of the universe. As the God of Israel, He is regarded as King of His people, even after the institution of the Israelite monarchy. Those who submit to Yahweh as King experience forgiveness of sin (Psalms 32; 130; Jeremiah 31:18), receive circumcision of heart and/or a new heart (Deuteronomy 30:6; 1 Samuel 10:9; Psalm 24:4; Jeremiah 24:5-7; Ezekiel 11:15-20; 18:27; 36:25), and are indwelt by the Holy Spirit (Psalm 51:11). At the same time, there grew out of God's marvelous promises to David a manifestation of a kingdom which would supersede its present dimension (Daniel 7). This hope opened up Israel's messianic expectation. By the first century, several groups of Jews were preoccupied with the relationship between the coming of the Messiah and the future dimension of God's kingdom.

Jesus and the Kingdom

The ministry of John the Baptist combined the tension between the present reality of God's kingdom and the expectation of an imminent manifestation of the Kingdom. On the one hand, John preached a conversion baptism. In the light of the coming judgment, men and women were instructed to convert (repent) and be baptized for the remission of sins. As a result of their faith, those responsive to John's preaching received forgiveness for their sins and were expected, through the enabling power of the Holy Spirit, to bring forth the fruit of conversion (Matthew 3:8; Luke 3:7-14). Simply put, John preached salvation.

On the other hand, it is clear that the Baptist anticipated a greater manifestation of the Kingdom through the coming of the Messiah. John envisioned the appearance of the Lord to bring both salvation and judgment. For already the ax is at the root of the tree and the winnowing fork is in His hand (Matthew 3:10, 12).

When Jesus began His public ministry, He proclaimed the kingdom of God (Mark 1:15). Jesus' entire ministry was a proclamation of God's kingdom, open to sinners who convert and hidden from those who do not believe. As His mission unfolded, it became obvious that Jesus himself was inextricably connected to the Kingdom and caused its fuller manifestation.

The Kingdom Is Present

The four Gospels are unanimous in their testimony that the Kingdom became a present reality through the life of Jesus:

• In response to a question concerning the arrival of the Kingdom, Jesus answered that the Kingdom is already among (or within) those who hear Him (Luke 17:20, 21).

• Because Jesus cast out demons by the Spirit of God, it was obvious that the kingdom of God

had come (Matthew 12:28).
- The miraculous works of Jesus testified of the Kingdom's presence. Jesus informed His disciples that it is the "Father's good pleasure to give" the Kingdom to His children (Luke 12:32).
- Jesus stated that prostitutes and tax collectors were already entering into the kingdom of God (Matthew 21:31).
- Jesus spoke to Nicodemus about entering the Kingdom through birth from above (John 3:5).

Whatever else may be said about the Kingdom, it is obvious that already in Jesus' earthly ministry the kingdom of God was present and that Jesus sought to extend the Kingdom through His life's work.

The Kingdom Is Future

In some ways, an even more intensive emphasis was placed on the future dimension of the Kingdom in the preaching of Jesus.
- Near the end of His earthly ministry, Jesus gave a discourse concerning future events. In this part of His teaching He often spoke about the coming of the Kingdom (Matthew 24, 25; Mark 13; Luke 21).
- Just before the Transfiguration, Jesus told His disciples that some of them would not die until they saw the kingdom of God coming in power (Mark 9:1).
- The sons of Zebedee requested seats of honor when Jesus' kingdom would be fully manifest (Matthew 20:21).
- At the Last Supper, Jesus said He would not partake of the fruit of the vine until He does so with the disciples in the Kingdom (Luke 22:18).

From these and other references it is possible to

discern the broad outline of this future Kingdom. There will come a day when Jesus will rule on the earth in fulfillment of the messianic promises of the Old Testament. As with the Old Testament idea of the Day of the Lord, this reign will involve judgment and rewards. The New Testament is clear about the inauguration of this dimension of the Kingdom—the return of Jesus.

Already but Not Yet

How can one make sense of what appears to be such contradictory evidence? What can account for Jesus' preaching both the presence of and the coming of the Kingdom? The most appropriate explanation is to acknowledge that the kingdom of God is already present but not yet fully present. That is to say, the Kingdom is clearly manifest (and much more clearly manifest than ever before); however, the full consummation of the Kingdom has not yet occurred.

The apostle Paul explained this phenomenon along the lines of the two ages: the present age of sin and death and the coming age of the Messiah. When Jesus came, He ushered in the new age. His resurrection is the firstfruits that ensures the future resurrection of believers (1 Corinthians 15:20). The Holy Spirit is the down payment of that which is to come (Ephesians 1:13, 14). In other words, the messianic age has come, but it has come only in part. Sin, disease, and death continue to be present in this time when the two ages overlap. Yet there is coming a day when this present evil age will pass away, the day when Jesus returns. At the Second Coming, the messianic age will be fully consummated. Death, disease, and sin will disappear. The Lord Jesus will reign over all. The Kingdom will be fully manifest.

The Nature of the Kingdom

Fundamental for understanding the nature of the Kingdom is the realization that the Kingdom belongs to God. It is His kingdom and is established because He desires its establishment. While human beings may have a part in the work of the Kingdom, it is absolutely beyond human abilities to usher in or bring to consummation the kingdom of God.

The manifestation of the Kingdom exhibits a mysterious quality. Most often, Jesus used parables to teach about the mystery of the Kingdom. Each of these parables explains a certain dimension of the Kingdom:

- The parable of the sower (Matthew 13:1-9, 18-23) reveals why certain groups of people fail to receive the gospel, while others enjoy astounding growth.
- The parable of the wheat and weeds (Matthew 13:24-30) suggests that final judgment concerning the identity of Kingdom members is left to God.
- The parable of the mustard seed (Matthew 13:31, 32) calls attention to the inconspicuous beginnings of the Kingdom and its inexplicable growth.
- The parable of the leaven (Matthew 13:33) sets forth the Kingdom's ability to affect the world and effect change, despite the Kingdom's relative obscurity.
- Other parables (Matthew 13:44-50) affirm the incomparable value of the Kingdom.

Membership in the Kingdom is also addressed. In order to become a member of the Kingdom, a birth from above (new birth) is essential (John 3:3, 5). No one can enter the Kingdom without this experience. In addition, those who enter must bear a cross (Matthew 16:24), give Jesus undivided allegiance (Matthew 10:37), and take responsibility for the poor and oppressed (Matthew 25:31-46). In light of the entrance requirement of regeneration along with these other stated characteristics, it is evident that the constituency of the Kingdom and the church are identical.

Conclusions and Implications

What are the implications of this study for the contemporary views concerning the kingdom of God? Three aspects are of particular significance.

First, two radically different misinterpretations have emerged from the dual nature of the Kingdom. On the one hand, an overemphasis on the present dimension of the Kingdom has led to a number of inaccurate deductions. For example, it is often claimed that the fullness of the Kingdom and its effects are already present. From this conclusion, it is further deduced that the effects of sin (disease, poverty, and oppression) are no longer operative. Consequently, it is claimed that Christians need never be sick, poor, or dominated by any force (political or otherwise). Instead, the believer should live above illness, poverty, and political oppression. In fact, Christians should expect their own efforts to bring about the establishment of the Kingdom on earth, the Millennium. In other words, the church is to usher in the Kingdom when Christ will rule personally. Apparently, the Corinthians made similar claims but were severely chastised by Paul for such an unbiblical emphasis (1 Corinthians 4:8-13). Such a view of the Kingdom fails to appreciate the biblical distinction between the present and future dimensions of the Kingdom. On the other hand, those who overemphasize the future aspect of the Kingdom fail to appreciate God's activity in the present. Often, such an emphasis leads to a rejection of God's miraculous activity today. This view restricts divine intervention to the New Testament period and to the time of Jesus' return. Again, such a position fails to distinguish properly between the two dimensions of the Kingdom.

Second, the realization that the Kingdom belongs to God has major implications for the accuracy of the concept of the Kingdom's role and status in a contemporary setting. Since the Kingdom has its origin in God and belongs to Him, it follows that only God can bring the Kingdom to its consummation. This understanding makes clear that while believers participate in the proclamation of the Kingdom, it is God who establishes the Kingdom, regardless of the cooperation of men and women. Consequently, those who suggest that the church will usher in the Millennium misunderstand the biblical teaching concerning the role of God and the church in relation to the consummation of the Kingdom.

Third, the mysterious nature of the Kingdom contributes to a proper understanding of the function of believers in the work of the Kingdom. Since God establishes His Kingdom, He may use anyone or anything in the process. No one is too small, weak, or unimportant to have part in this divine work. Just as the mustard seed produces a structure unbelievably larger than itself, God uses weak and foolish vessels in His kingdom's work. Because the function of the Kingdom in the world is much like the work of leaven in a batch of dough, it is unwise to calculate the strength of the Kingdom on the basis of external structures and institutions. This statement is true for at least two reasons: (1) Not everything which appears to be wheat is wheat; weeds are still present. (2) The influence of Kingdom members is far more extensive than appears on the surface. Therefore, the church should not give in to the temptation to judge its success by the building of large state-of-the-art structures or its respectability in various social circles. Such an assessment is clearly out of harmony with the message of the parables about the Kingdom.

The kingdom of God is a present reality which utilizes believers in its work. This work involves proclamation, holiness, battle against the powers of Satan, and care for the helpless and the oppressed. Although God reigns in the present, the Kingdom member is not exempt from certain consequences which result from living in a fallen world. At the return of Jesus, however, the last vestiges of satanic power will be destroyed and the Kingdom will be established in its fullness.

CHAPTER 4

RIGHTEOUS LIVING: A NEW TESTAMENT PERSPECTIVE

What does it mean to live a righteous life? This question is often answered by using the term *perfection*. After all, Jesus said, "Be perfect, therefore, as your heavenly Father is perfect" (Matthew 5:48, *NIV*). But what did Jesus mean when He said, "Be perfect"? To understand this verse, one must be aware of why Jesus said these words when He did.

The theme discussed in Matthew 5:38-48 is love. Jesus informed His disciples that in His kingdom personal injury is no longer to be repaid by retaliation. Instead, the believer is to exhibit a loving and caring attitude toward those very individuals who would be considered enemies. Jesus mentioned turning the other cheek, going an extra mile, and giving to those who ask. However, these are merely examples of the kinds of actions which result when one loves. These responses are unexpected. This action transcends the types of responses common in human relationships.

Such behavior demonstrates that one is a child of God. For God loves the just and the unjust. He sends the sun and the rain to both. Regardless of an individual's standing before Him, God is generous in His provisions to all. In other words, He loves those whom no one else loves. He cares for those who do not deserve such affection. God's love is available not only for His children but also to men and women who refuse to recognize Him as Lord.

There is no reward for loving those who reciprocate love. Even the hated tax collectors had the ability to love those who loved them. Rather, the follower of Jesus is to exhibit a genuine love both for fellow Christians and for those who care little for God and His cause. In doing this, the believer acts as a child of God ought to act.

Therefore, perfection must be understood in the context of love. The Greek word that is translated "perfect" (τέλειος) carries the meaning of wholeness or completeness. In other words, Jesus instructed His disciples to be complete in loving other people, whether they deserve it or not, just as the heavenly Father is complete in His love. Consequently, love becomes a family trait, passed on from the Father to the child. If one is God's child, love must be present in that one's life. Here, then, perfection means loving as God loves.

But can such a thing be achieved? No doubt, most Christians have had the unhappy experience of trying but failing to love those who seem unlovable. Probably, one reason this is hard to accomplish is that the *Christian* tries to do it. According to Paul (Galatians 5:22, 23), love, joy, peace, patience, kindness, goodness, faithfulness, gentleness, and self-control are fruit of the Spirit. These are not accomplished by human ingenuity but are cultivated by the Holy Spirit in the life of the maturing Christian. All aspects of the fruit of the Spirit are to be exhibited in every believer. They, as those qualities discussed in the Beatitudes (Matthew 5:3-12), are not descriptions of different kinds of Christians; rather, they describe one believer from different perspectives. These characteristics are grown and developed in the life of those who nurture their spiritual relationship with God. They cannot be artificially produced.

Therefore, righteous living has to do with authentic growth in our walk with God. It means becoming so like our Father that His characteristics are present in our lives. This results in our reflecting His love and concern for those around us. "Be perfect, therefore, as your heavenly Father is perfect" (*NIV*).

FOOTWASHING: ITS PRACTICE AND MEANING

Of the Church of God's many distinctive beliefs and practices, that of washing the saints' feet in worship continues to be among the most misunderstood and neglected. Many congregations in the denomination rarely observe the rite; and when footwashing is scheduled as part of a worship service, attendance is significantly lower than usual.

Perhaps the most significant factor in footwashing's decline in our ranks is a common assumption that because of its status as an ancient Oriental custom, footwashing should at best be regarded as a culturally conditioned sign of humility or service. The implication is that since Jesus used it as a mere example of

humility or service, He certainly did not intend for the
later church to practice footwashing. Instead, the
church should seek to appropriate contemporary
signs of humility or service in order to fulfill the commands of Jesus to wash one another's feet. If correct,
this line of interpretation naturally leads to a de-
emphasis of the practice of footwashing. But is such
an interpretation in line with the intention of Jesus in
John 13? Or has this understanding been superim-
posed on the text because for many in the Western
world the idea of washing one another's feet has a
foreign or even primitive sound to it?

In confronting this cultural argument, Pentecostals
know very well that a number of things in Scripture
which others consider to be obsolete are still part of
God's plan for the church. In other words,
Pentecostals are not generally inclined to give up a
practice commanded in Scripture simply because it
does not appear to be part of their culture's experience. The real issue should be, what does the
Scripture say about this practice of footwashing?

Should the Church Practice Footwashing?

When Jesus washed the feet of His disciples, He
took a step that was shocking in the ancient world.
There is no evidence to support that any person of
superior status, with the exception of Jesus, ever voluntarily washed the feet of a subordinate. Shortly
after rendering this service, Jesus gave His disciples
rather explicit commands to wash one another's feet:

> "If, therefore, I your Lord and Teacher have
> washed your feet, you also are obligated to wash
> one another's feet. For I have given you an exam-

ple in order that you should do just as I have done. Truly, truly, I say to you, no servant is greater than his Lord, neither is a sent one greater than the one who sends. If you know these things, blessed are you if you do them" (John 13:14-17).

For several reasons it appears that Jesus' words should be taken as calling for a literal compliance. *The most natural reading of the text is one which calls for a literal fulfillment.* Not only did Jesus' completely unexpected example suggest that He was serious about the practice, but He also made this intention explicit by the language He used. Jesus said that the disciples were obligated to wash one another's feet. Whenever this verb appears in John's writings it indicates an obligation, not simply a suggestion or good idea (cf. John 19:7; 1 John 2:6; 3:16; 4:11; 3 John 8).

The word translated "example" in John 13:15 does not convey the idea of moral example as much as it does "prototype" or "illustration" of how something is to be done, as it meant in Greek medical manuals of the day. Jesus said those who know *and* do these things are blessed (v. 17). Amazingly, neither the rites of baptism or the Lord's Supper are given such explicit words of institution in the New Testament.

Both the disciples described in John 13 and the readers for whom the Gospel of John was written would have had little reason to interpret the commands in anything other than a literal fashion. The Hebrew Scriptures contain numerous references to footwashing. In preparation for entrance into certain sections of the Tabernacle and Temple, the priests were instructed to wash their hands and feet (Exodus

30:17-21; 40:30-32; 2 Chronicles 4:6). Several Old Testament passages present washing the feet as a part of personal hygiene and comfort (2 Samuel 11:8-11; 19:24; Song of Songs 5:3). In other biblical references, footwashing is offered to guests by a host/hostess as an act of hospitality (Genesis 18:4; 19:2; 24:32; 43:24; Judges 19:21; 1 Samuel 25:41).

Other evidence demonstrates that footwashing was offered to banquet guests in particular (Luke 7:44; see also *Testament of Abraham* 3:6-9; *Joseph and Asenath* 20; *Plutarch's Life of Phocion* 20:2; Herodotus, Book II: 72). Ordinarily, one invited to a banquet would bathe at home, needing only to wash the feet when arriving at the home of the host/hostess to remove the dust and debris accumulated on the journey. Since footwashing was such a part of their everyday life, their most natural hearing of these words would be understood to call for a literal observance.

That the commands to wash feet were intended to be taken literally is shown by the way the earliest readers of John's Gospel interpreted the commands. In point of fact, the vast majority of the early church who commented on John 13:14-17 understood the words of Jesus as calling for a literal fulfillment. First Timothy 5:10 demonstrates that late in Paul's life, the church had not forgotten this command of our Lord. In this passage the feet of the saints were to be washed by a group (or order) of widows. It is significant that "washing the saints' feet" is listed with other good works: child rearing, hospitality, and helping those in need.

Two things of importance should be noted about this verse. First, it is the feet of the saints which were to be washed, not people in general. Second, footwashing is distinguished from hospitality in the list of

1 Timothy 5:10. These considerations seem to confirm that footwashing was no longer thought of in terms of hospitality but was given spiritual significance. Other interpreters who advocate the continuation of the practice include Tertullian (*De Corona* 8), John Chrysostom (*Homilies on John* 71), Ambrose (*Of the Holy Spirit* 1.15), Augustine (*John: Tractate* 58.4), John Cassian (*Institute of Coenobia* 4:19), and Caesarius of Arles (*Sermon* 203). In the light of this evidence it seems safe to conclude that Jesus intended to institute footwashing as an ongoing practice of the church.

What Is the Meaning of Footwashing?

If the text of John 13 makes clear that Jesus meant for footwashing to be continued by His disciples, what was its intended meaning? Several aspects of this passage make explicit that the footwashing Jesus instituted was no ordinary footwashing.

In a variety of ways John made clear that the footwashing was connected to the passion and death of Jesus. This act occurs in the first part of John 13—17, the portion of the Gospel devoted to a description of Jesus' preparing His disciples for His departure. In John 13:1 the reader is told that Jesus' hour had finally come. It was His hour of exaltation on the cross, and the reader is told that He loved His own until the end. His return to the Father, mentioned in verse 3, also connects the footwashing with His passion, as does the appearance of Judas the betrayer in verse 2. Finally, several scholars see a reference to the death of Jesus in verse 4, where He is described as laying aside His clothing, since when John uses the Greek term meaning "to lay aside," it ordinarily has reference to Jesus' death.

Another indication that there is more to this foot-washing than meets the eye is the fact that it is chronologically out of place. When a footwashing occurred in the context of a meal in the ancient world, it preceded the meal, most often occurring at the door of the host. However, the footwashing which Jesus enacted interrupted the meal, rather than preceded it. Thus, this footwashing is underscored by its unusual placement.

That this footwashing is unusual is indicated also by the highly deliberative way in which Jesus' actions are described. Instead of simply saying that Jesus washed the feet of the disciples, John methodically under-scored the significance of Jesus' actions by specifically mentioning each step of the procedure (vv. 4, 5).

Verse 7 indicates that this footwashing was no ordinary one when Jesus himself informed Peter that he would not understand the significance of His action until after these things. Just as the disciples were unable to comprehend other events recorded in the Fourth Gospel fully until after the Resurrection (John 2:22; 12:16), so Peter and the other disciples with him were unable to understand the full significance of footwashing until after the Resurrection.

In responding to Peter's emphatic rejection of the footwashing (v. 8), Jesus informed Peter that this act is not optional and that its significance is far-reaching. "If I do not wash you, you have no part [or share] with me." According to the Gospel of John, to have a share in Jesus' destiny includes not only eternal life but also . . .

- being sent as Jesus himself was sent (4:31-38; 20:21-23)

- being resurrected at the last day (6:40)
- being hated by the world (15:18-16:4).

Simply put, Peter was told that his continued fellowship with Jesus was dependent upon his participation in the washing Jesus offers.

Finally, the primary meaning of the footwashing is given in John 13:10. In response to Peter's request for washings in addition to his feet, Jesus said, "The one who has bathed has no need to wash except the feet; but is wholly clean; and you are clean, though not all of you." Three things are worth noting here:

1. Two different words are used for *wash* in this verse. *Bathe* means a complete bath; *wash* is used to denote partial washings such as the hands, face, or feet.

2. Jesus made reference to a *bath* which Peter had already received. Given the narrative of the Gospel, the only possible meaning of *bath* to this point is the water baptism administered by John the Baptist (1:26; 3:23), Jesus (3:22; 4:1), and the disciples (4:2).

3. Jesus made an identification between footwashing and the cleansing from sin which believers contract through daily life in this world. Just as a banquet guest would bathe at home and wash only the feet at the house of the host or hostess to remove the dust and debris accumulated on the road, so Peter, and the believer who experiences baptism, which signifies a complete cleansing from sin, does not need to be rebaptized but undergoes footwashing which signifies the removal of sin that might accumulate as a result of life in this sinful world.

In a sense, then, footwashing is an extension of baptism, for it signifies the washing away of postconversion sins in the believer's life, a concern emphatically displayed in John's later epistle (see 1 John 1:8—2:2; 5:16-18).

Footwashing, then, is a sacrament on the same level as the Lord's Supper and Water Baptism. It is given eternal significance by Jesus, who commands that it be continued in the church. The meaning of footwashing is not to be found primarily in terms of humility or service but in the sacrificial death of our Lord.

When the church participates in footwashing, a number of important aspects of worship are present:

1. There is a remembrance of Jesus' own actions in preparing the disciples for His departure, just before His sacrificial death.

2. Footwashing serves as a constant reminder of the continual forgiveness available to the believer, who travels in this sinful world.

3. The benefits of water baptism are extended in this action. Just as water baptism signifies the washing away of sin committed before conversion, so footwashing signifies the cleansing from sin that might be committed after conversion.

4. The various members of the body work together in rendering and receiving footwashing.

How Should Footwashing Be Practiced Today?

There are a variety of appropriate contexts for the practice of footwashing in the ministry of the church today. Given its placement in the Gospel of John, the most suitable context for footwashing would be just before the Lord's Supper. This would function in accord with Paul's admonition for self-examination before approaching the Lord's Table (see 1 Corinthians

11:27-34). As a sign of cleansing from sin, footwashing could help recover and reappropriate confession (James 5:16) and forgiveness in many church communities where little or no place has been given for such activities.

When a church has not practiced footwashing for some time, perhaps the best place to begin would be for the pastor, as part of the Lord's Supper celebration, to call one or more people forward; and while John 13:1-17 is being read, the pastor could wash the feet of these individuals before the congregation. Such a model would be a powerful sign to the church and help prompt others to participate.

Other appropriate settings for footwashing include hospital visitation (especially for those with life-threatening illnesses), pastoral counseling (particularly as a sign of closure and cleansing for victims of sexual abuse), commissioning and ordination services (for various aspects of ministry service), and periods of reconciliation (as an instrument to bring together those who are estranged from one another).

Conclusion

For nearly two decades I have made an in-depth study of footwashing. In that time I have witnessed firsthand—and heard many testimonies about—the way God has worked among His people through the practice of footwashing. There have been testimonies of healing, reconciliation, forgiveness, encouragement, and sanctification. At the final official gathering of the Pentecostal Fellowship of North America, which included Pentecostal groups which do not ordinarily practice footwashing, two separate spontaneous footwashings took place between black and white leaders as signs of forgiveness and reconciliation. By all accounts, these actions were two of the most significant events to take place at this historic meeting. Might we Pentecostals be encountering the very thing that Jesus put before the disciples in John 13—an inspired call over against the customs of the day to take up the literal act of washing another's feet? The power of this sign, which was instituted by Jesus himself, is hard to overestimate. May we have the courage to retain its practice in order that the life of the church might be strengthened and that we might be obedient to our Lord who has commanded it!

JESUS AND THE FAMILY

The centrality of the person of Jesus for Christian faith hardly needs emphasis, for His importance as a model for Christian belief and practice is unrivaled. Because of His unquestioned position as Lord of the church, one expects to find a great deal of attention paid to Jesus' attitudes and actions relating to significant contemporary issues facing the church. Quite surprisingly, this strategic aspect of biblical inquiry is many times lacking. Two examples should demonstrate the accuracy of this observation.

First, for the past few years the Church of God, along with many other denominations, has been considering the biblical role and function of women in the body of Christ. Most of the attention has been focused on a couple of passages in the Pauline literature, with little or no consideration of Jesus' own attitude toward women and His view of their place in Kingdom work.

A second illustration concerns the AIDS crisis. While many Christians have been quick to identify this epidemic as a God-sent curse on the homosexual community, no one seems to be raising the question, how would Jesus treat an AIDS victim? An interesting comparison may be made with a highly feared disease of Jesus' day, leprosy. As is AIDS, leprosy was thought to be highly contagious. It rendered one ceremonially unclean, and its victim could not go to the Temple. The leprous condition was widely interpreted as punishment for sin. Most lepers were isolated from the rest of society, waiting to die. Despite these conditions and attitudes, Jesus violated social norms by going to victims of leprosy and touching them. In both of these cases, there is much to be learned from the example of Jesus.

The present interest in the family among a variety of Christians makes it worthwhile to examine Jesus' attitude toward the family. Despite the fact that little attention has been given to this topic, there is a great deal of material and many points of connection between Jesus and the family. In fact, there is so much information that one must choose between an in-depth analysis of one or two significant passages or offer a survey of the diverse material. Perhaps it is best to opt for the broader approach, given the lack of attention given to the topic. Consequently, the methodology of this study is to survey the biblical material relevant to the topic. The final section is devoted to principles and issues from this material which are of significance for the Pentecostal family in particular.

Jesus' Family

The obvious starting point is to identify and examine Jesus' family members and His relationship with them. There are three important components: Jesus' relationship with and views on His parents, His siblings, and marriage.

Jesus' Parents. Because of the unique nature of Jesus' conception and birth, most attention has been focused on Mary and the virginal conception through the agency of the Holy Spirit. In fact, it is not uncommon to find little concern or appreciation for the role Joseph served in Jesus' life. Yet Joseph's position and function were quite strategic.

Only two of the four canonical Gospels, Matthew and Luke, include accounts of Jesus' birth. While Luke related the story with special interest in Mary and her function, Matthew had an intense interest in Joseph. This interest was due, in part, to Matthew's desire to establish Jesus as the Davidic Messiah. In the genealogy with which Matthew opens his Gospel, the place of David is given much emphasis. Matthew appears to be listing those individuals who were, or would have been, the legitimate heir to the Davidic throne. Joseph is described as standing within this Davidic line.

As the story unfolds, Joseph is at center stage. He is seen in the first phase of marriage with a young woman named Mary, who was found to be pregnant. Joseph, a righteous and godly man, did not wish to put her to public shame, as society treated prostitutes and other sexually promiscuous women. Instead, he was willing to forgo the protection of witnesses afforded him by the Torah, in order to divorce her quietly and without fanfare. In the midst of contemplating his actions, Joseph received the first of three angelic visitations. The angel gave Joseph three directives: First, he was to complete the second phase of the Jewish marriage by "taking" Mary (from her father's house) to his home. Second, Joseph was told that Mary's condition was the result of the Holy Spirit's involvement. Third, Joseph was instructed that *he* was to name the baby. By naming the child, Joseph would acknowledge that Jesus was his legitimate heir and, therefore, would be recognized as a legal descendant of David.

Matthew was deliberative in describing Joseph's response after the angel's departure. Matthew said that Joseph did exactly what he was instructed to do (1:24, 25). He took Mary to his home, he did not tamper with the Holy Spirit's work by having sexual relations with Mary until after the birth, and he named the child Jesus.

Later, after the wise men returned to the East, an angel again appeared to Joseph, instructing him to take the child and his mother to Egypt and remain there until the Lord informed him that it was safe to return to Israel. Matthew 2:14, 15 describes Joseph's doing exactly as he was told, taking the mother and child to Egypt and waiting there. Joseph's earlier action ensured Jesus' legal place in the Davidic line. Now his actions preserved the life of the child Messiah as well as fulfilled Scripture.

The next mention of Joseph (Matthew 2:19) finds him patiently waiting in Egypt just as he had been instructed to do. Again the angel appeared to Joseph. This time he was commanded to take the child and His mother into the land of Israel. Verse 21 makes clear that Joseph again did exactly what the angel said. Verses 22 and 23 demonstrate Joseph's discernment in that he settled in one particular portion of the land of Israel, Nazareth. This settlement also fulfilled the Scripture.

The only other mention of Joseph comes in Luke's account of Jesus in the Temple at the age of 12. Because there are no other references to Joseph after this point, most scholars speculate that Joseph died sometime between the time Jesus was 12 and the beginning of His public ministry. Therefore, Jesus spent at least a few of His years without benefit of His "father."

The story of Jesus' mother is well-known. An angel appeared to a young virgin with the astonishing news that she was to bear a child through the Holy Spirit. Several aspects of Mary's role ought to be emphasized here. First is her willingness to be used by God in this unique way. Mary was obedient to the Lord even though she would endure much hardship because of her commitment. Second, throughout Jesus' childhood and early ministry, Mary proved to have been a reflective person. On several occasions she is described as pondering the significance of particular acts and events. Third, Mary was supportive of Jesus' ministry, although at times she attempted to dictate His action (John 2:1-5) or to intervene on His behalf (Mark 3:21). Yet she was faithful to the end; she was present at the Crucifixion, at the tomb, at the Resurrection, and on the Day of Pentecost. Mary exhibited a loving, caring attitude toward her son and the ability to relate to Him on a different level when He made the demands of discipleship clear.

Jesus' Siblings. There has been quite a bit of controversy concerning the New Testament statements which affirm that Jesus had both brothers and sisters.

From at least the middle of the second century, there were Christians who took the biblical statements about Jesus' brothers and sisters as having reference to Joseph's children by a previous marriage. This interpretation sought to harmonize references to Jesus' siblings with the theological conviction that Mary was a virgin her entire life.

As veneration for virginity and celibacy increased in the early church, another interpretation of the brothers and sisters arose. In the late fourth century, Jerome argued that these terms are best understood as meaning cousins. In other words, Jerome felt that both Mary and Joseph were perpetual virgins. The obvious problem with Jerome's view is that while the meaning of the Greek term (ἀδελφὸς) could possibly be stretched to have this meaning, there is a perfectly good New Testament word for *cousin*. Obviously, both these views seem motivated by theological convictions rather than a straightforward reading of the text. In fact, the New Testament seems to indicate that there were children born to Mary and Joseph after the birth of Jesus.

The New Testament gives little information about the sisters of Jesus except to affirm their existence. There is no mention of their names, and it is not even clear how many sisters Jesus had. Mark 6:3 makes reference to them and seems to imply that they married and settled in Nazareth.

More information is available about Jesus' brothers. For one thing, their names have been preserved in Mark 6:3: James, Joses, Jude (Judah), and Simon. They appear to have followed Jesus from time to time (see Mark 3:21, 31) but apparently did not believe in Him until after Jesus' resurrection. John 7:1-9 indicates that their unbelief was expressed in the form of a challenge. They wanted Jesus to go up to Jerusalem for the Feast of Tabernacles and exhibit miraculous powers. It was not until after the Resurrection that they believed.

It appears likely that James believed as a result of a post-Resurrection appearance from Jesus (1 Corinthians 15:7). Later, James became the leader of the Jerusalem church, writing at least one epistle and an encyclical sent to the church, containing the decision of the Jerusalem Council. An examination of the Epistle of James reveals a very close affinity with Jesus' teachings as recorded in Matthew's Gospel. In addition to James, Jude (the Lord's brother) is thought by many to have written a letter to the church about the dangers of false teaching. This information about Jesus' brothers and sisters makes clear that He was no hermit but grew up in the context of family life.

Two other details should be mentioned before leaving this section of the study. First, Luke observed that Jesus was related to John the Baptist. However, it is difficult to determine the extent of their contact before Jesus' baptism, for there is no hint in the baptism account that they knew one another. Such a situation might be explained by the fact that John's parents were advanced in years at his birth. If they died when he was quite young, perhaps John was adopted by someone else.[1]   Second, it is sometimes suggested that Jesus was related to the Beloved Disciple, described in the Fourth Gospel.

Jesus and Marriage.   It is sometimes argued that Jesus himself was married. Such a belief is a little-known aspect of Mormon doctrine, but it is also occasionally asserted by more mainstream advocates. While most people would dismiss this possibility as the outlandish claims of some fringe group or publicity-hungry scholar, perhaps the question should be addressed at this point.

A couple of pieces of evidence are offered in favor of the claim.   First, a study of Hebrew marital customs in the first century reveals that most Jews followed the command recorded in Genesis 1:28:   "Be fruitful and multiply."   This command was taken with utmost sincerity.   Second, when compared with the more ascetic John the Baptist, it is obvious that Jesus was much more representative of His culture concerning contact with the opposite sex.   While these observations are true, such circumstantial evidence hardly builds a strong case that Jesus was married.

Of those who claim that Jesus was married, there is near unanimity concerning the identity of His "wife." Mary Magdalene is alleged to be the most likely candidate. If true, this point would explain why Jesus appeared to her first on the day of His resurrection.

However, there is, in fact, *no* direct evidence concerning His marital status. While it is theoretically

---

[1]The group of Essenes who lived at Qumran is the most likely candidate, owing to the similarities between their theology and John's as well as the fact that Essenes did adopt orphan boys on occasion.

possible that Jesus may have been married, it is not probable that He was. The lack of supporting evidence in this case is decisive, because the early church gave honor to Jesus' family members very soon after His departure. James became the leader of the church in Jerusalem, Mary's veneration is well documented in later history, and according to Eusebius (*Ecclesiastical History*, Book III: 20) even Jude's grandchildren were revered at the turn of the first and second centuries. If Jesus had been married, it is nearly impossible to believe that there is absolutely no evidence of it in early Christianity.

Jesus' Attitude Toward the Family

Jesus' Attitude Toward Parents. On two different occasions Jesus reemphasized the teaching of the Torah concerning honor to be given father and mother. When the rich young man asked how he might inherit eternal life (Mark 10:17-22), Jesus responded by citing examples of the Ten Words (Commandments). One of these examples was "Honor your father and mother." On another occasion when describing the future, He said that children will rebel against their parents and have them put to death (Mark 13:12). Such atrocity seems impossible to believe. Obviously, Jesus viewed these actions as sinful.

Jesus' affirmation of honor toward parents was more than just quoting from the Ten Words. He expected that such honor would be lived out in tangible ways. In responding to the preoccupation with ritual purity (washing the hands) on the part of certain Pharisees and teachers of the Law, Jesus challenged the practice of Corban mentioned in Mark 7:9-13. To declare something Corban was to restrict its use from its original purpose. Although this declaration implied the Corban item would be dedicated to Yahweh, it did not always entail such a use. Ordinarily, a vow of Corban affected the owner, but sometimes could be used to affect someone else. In fact, at times this oath could be made in anger, so that it was uttered out of spite.

The main issue for the Pharisees on this occasion was the irreversibility of oaths. In the case that Jesus cited, a man, apparently in haste and anger, cursed his parents by declaring that the support they should be able to expect from their heirs would be unavailable to them. Jesus classified such teaching (oral tradition or interpretation) as an illegitimate attempt to invalidate the words of Moses. For the purpose of this study, the main point is that one must fulfill his or her obligations and duties to one's parents as the Torah instructs. No interpretive maneuvering could change that. In addition, note the strong language used to describe the curse on those who break this command (v. 10).

Therefore, Jesus' attitude toward parents was one which upheld the sacred relationship the Torah sets forth.

Jesus' Attitude Toward Children. The Graeco-Roman attitude toward children was quite different from that of Jews and Christians. For example, both abortion and death of infants by exposure were practiced in the Gentile world with little moral concern. While children were valued in Judaism, their place was somewhat restricted. Jesus exhibited a radically different attitude toward children.

Mark 9:33-37 describes a discussion between Jesus and the disciples about greatness. This issue was often discussed in first-century Palestine, for honor and greatness were coveted. (One issue of contention was the order in which people would be seated at a banquet.) Jesus turned things upside down by stating that in His kingdom the servant would be the greatest of all. Taking a child in His arms, Jesus said, "Whoever receives one of these little children in My name receives me" (Mark 9:37).

Using the illustration of a child, Jesus made two points. First, He emphasized the fact that even those regarded as small or insignificant are in reality very important in the Kingdom. They are worth investing in and receiving. Second, Jesus' identification with children is comforting. This association in itself underscores His positive attitude toward children.

On another occasion, people (fathers or older children) were bringing children for Jesus to bless—literally, "to touch" (Luke 18:15-17). The disciples, not wanting Jesus to be troubled, rebuked these actions. This rebuke upset Jesus to the point of indignation. He forbade anyone to interfere with the children; He affirmed their place in the Kingdom; He asserted that no one is able to receive the Kingdom unless it's as a child receives; Jesus touched, held, and blessed the children. One of the main emphases of this passage is upon how one must receive the gift of the Kingdom. However, several things may be deduced from it about Jesus' attitude toward children:

1. Jesus made it clear that children are not to be relegated to those with more time and less importance. He himself took time for them. By rebuking the disciples, He was complimenting those who brought the children to Him.

2. He again made clear that the Kingdom is for

those who have no claims on it: the weak, the poor, and the powerless. Consequently, time devoted to children is time well invested.

3. Jesus taught as much by His actions as His words. Instead of brushing the children aside, He communicated love and affection.

It might be worthwhile to compare Jesus' loving actions with a somewhat typical attitude toward children exhibited in the Greek papyri. Adolf Deissmann has published a letter from Egypt in which a husband wrote to his pregnant wife, "I pray of you and exhort you, take care of the little child. . . . If you are delivered, if it is a male child, let it [live]; if it is female, cast it out."[2]

Jesus' Attitude Toward Marriage. The attitude Jesus exhibited toward marriage may be discerned through several passages. John's account of the wedding at Cana (2:1-11) is a natural place to begin. The story is well known, if for no other reason than that it was there Jesus turned water into wine. Both Jesus and His disciples had been invited to the wedding, evidently on a prosperous estate (the presence of servants suggests this interpretation). By accepting the invitation, Jesus not only gave His implicit approval to marriage, but it seems He was also acknowledging this part of human experience as especially important. There is no hint whatever that Jesus harbored any misgivings about the institution of marriage. In fact, the miracle He performed facilitated the celebration itself. (It should not be overlooked that as a result of this first miracle His glory was revealed to the disciples and called forth faith on their part). This

---

[2]Adolf Deissmann, *Light From the Ancient East* (trans., L.R.M. Strachan; Grand Rapids: Baker, 1978), pp. 167-170.

event in and of itself is enough to indicate Jesus' high view of marriage, but there is more.

Jesus also exhibited His appreciation of marriage through his strong denunciation of divorce. Several New Testament passages record Jesus' words about marriage and divorce (Matthew 5:27-32; 19:3-9; Mark 10:2-12; Luke 16:18). While there is some disagreement over how to interpret the phrase "except for *porneia*," (Matthew 19:9), there is absolutely no mistaking the fact that Jesus did not view marriage as something to be easily dissolved. His words declare that the hardness of men's hearts had brought about the concession of divorce. The implication is obvious; marriage was ordained by God to be indissoluble. Describing the origin of marriage as divine, Jesus demonstrated His own high regard for marriage.

Mention should also be made of those passages in which Jesus used various aspects of marriage as an analogy to explain portions of His ministry. In Mark 2:19, 20 He said, "How can the guests of the bridegroom fast while he is with them? They cannot, so long as they have him with them. But the time will come when the bridegroom will be taken from them, and on that day they will fast." Note also the context of the parable of the ten virgins (Matthew 25:1-13). The eschatological setting points to Jesus' return. There can be little doubt as to the identity of the bridegroom.[3]

Radical Redefinition of the Family in the Light of the Kingdom of God

With few exceptions, these observations are what one could expect in describing Jesus and the family.

---

[3]See also the parable of the Wedding Banquet in Matthew 22:1-14.

However, it is precisely at this juncture that things become problematic. The Gospels record a number of Jesus' sayings about the family that are, indeed, troublesome. To these sayings this chapter now turns.

Unless you hate your father and mother. . . . In the midst of a discussion on the cost of discipleship, Jesus uttered one of His most difficult statements about the family: "If anyone comes to me and does not hate [μισεῖ] his father and mother, his wife and children, his brothers and sisters—yes, even his own life—he cannot be my disciple" (Luke 14:26, *NIV*).

Talk of "hating" family members is quite upsetting to those who tend to interpret Scripture in a literal fashion. These words produce shock and fear, because they appear to be diametrically opposed to other passages where Jesus affirmed one's duty to parents, children, and spouse. Before attempting to reconcile these passages, it should be noted that the tension itself may be the key to making these apparently contradictory emphases comprehensible. In other words, Jesus intended these words to call forth in the hearer the exact response that it does produce. Therefore, the first step in their interpretation is to acknowledge that these words hit the mark and cause a great deal of consternation. But exactly what did Jesus mean in Luke 14:26?

In the Old Testament, "to hate" could be used as a form of comparison in discussing affection. To love one person and hate another was a figure of speech which meant that an individual loved one person more than another person. It did not mean necessarily that hate was felt or expressed (see Deuteronomy 21:15). Apparently, Luke used this same idiom in Luke 14:26, for Matthew recorded the same statement by Jesus as follows: "Anyone who loves [φιλῶν] his father or mother more than me is not worthy of me; anyone who loves his son or daughter more than me is not worthy of me" (10:37, *NIV*).

Clearly, Jesus was saying that it is possible for family to stand in the way of one's fulfilling the Kingdom's call. While the New Testament affirms some accommodation, there may be those times when families will be divided physically because of the Kingdom. Mark 10:17-31 testifies to the fact that some of Jesus' disciples had experienced just such separation. The intent of Jesus' discussion about hating one's parents is to drive home the point that answering the call of God takes precedence over all other relationships.

Leave the dead to bury their own dead. One of the most astounding remarks of Jesus takes place in the context of the call to discipleship. He called one man who asked to be excused until he could go bury his father. Jesus replied, "Let the dead bury their own dead, but you go and proclaim the kingdom of God" (Luke 9:60, *NIV*).

In the first century, burial of the dead was regarded as an act of righteous living. It was so important that even though contact with a corpse would cause one to be declared ceremonially unclean (disqualifying one from Temple participation), the duty overrode the liability. Due to the command to honor father and mother, burial of one's parents was even more important. How could Jesus be in such open disagreement with the teaching and implications of the Torah?

Because His command has been deemed too harsh, various explanations have been offered to soften the impact. Some, for example, suggest that the man's father was not yet dead. Others have sought to alleviate the difficulty by interpreting Jesus' words to mean: "Leave the dead [the morticians] to bury their dead." But such thinking does not appear to be the clear implications of Jesus' words.

The purpose of these radical words is similar to the statement about hating one's father and mother. That is, the goal of the saying is to make clear that Jesus' call supersedes all other obligations, even those inferred from the Torah. Although most of us are repelled by the harsh tone of this command, the pages of missionary history are filled with examples of individuals who did exactly what Jesus required.

Call no man father. Still another difficult saying of Jesus is recorded in Matthew 23:9. Here Jesus said, "And do not call anyone on earth 'father,' for you have one Father, and he is in heaven"(*NIV*). Anyone who has taught a Sunday school class when this passage has been part of the text knows of the interesting discussions it generates and the sense of embarrassment it provokes, because most continue to call or refer to one's male parent as father. There are those, however, who seek to live by the letter of the law on this point and try to avoid calling anyone father. I have been instructed, on more than one occasion, by godly elders to cease calling my dad "father."

But what did Jesus mean? The context of this statement is Matthew 23, where a number of woes are directed from Jesus to the Pharisees. Among the practices He denounced is the love the Pharisees had for titles of honor. Jesus said His disciples should not strive to be called rabbi, master, father, or teacher.

Instead one should exhibit the humility of a servant in one's leadership patterns. All these titles were in use at this time, especially when Matthew's Gospel was written. Perhaps the nearest contemporary analogy is those who love to be called doctor or to be referred to by their title rather than be known as brother or sister. It is the craving for honor through one's title that Jesus seems to forbid, not reference to those who function in certain ways. As evidence, one should note that Paul could refer to himself as a father in the faith (1 Corinthians 4:15).

Who is my family? On one occasion the mother and brothers of Jesus came to a house where He was teaching and sent word for Him to come outside. At that point, Mark records, "'Who are my mother and my brothers?' he asked. Then he looked at those seated in a circle around him and said, 'Here are my mother and my brothers! Whoever does God's will is my brother and sister and mother'" (3:33-35, *NIV*).

This passage teaches us at least two important truths.

First, Jesus redefined the family in a radical fashion. Former relationships mean little and are not binding when the kingdom of God comes. This demand is similar to other words of Jesus—God's call overrides all other calls. Those who do God's will find that when they have lost family for the gospel's sake, they are rewarded with a multitude of mothers, brothers, sisters, and so forth, in the Kingdom (Mark 10:28-31).

Second, in Christ Jesus there is no room for relying on any relationship except the spiritual one. After the resurrection, Jesus' physical family seems to have learned this lesson. Notice that James referred to himself as the servant of Jesus, not the brother of Jesus

(1:1). This special bond between the people of God is evidenced by the fact that many Christians are closer to their spiritual families than their physical families.

Eunuchs for the Kingdom. On the heels of the discussion about divorce, some of the disciples concluded that it would be better not to marry at all. Jesus responded, "Not everyone can accept this word, but only those to whom it has been given. For some are eunuchs because they were born that way; others were made that way by men; and others have made themselves eunuchs because of the kingdom of heaven. The one who can accept this should accept it" (Matthew 19:11, 12, *NIV*).

The role of the eunuch was well known in the first-century world. The eunuch was many times given sensitive responsibilities, especially in matters involving the opposite sex, because his physical impairment rendered him sexually deficient. Jesus spoke of three categories of eunuchs: (1) males born without genitals, (2) men who have been castrated against their will, and (3) those who make themselves eunuchs for the Kingdom's sake. Eusebius reports that Origen took this passage very literally and made himself a eunuch (*Ecclesiastical History VI*, viii, 2).

However, it appears that Jesus was referring to celibacy in this passage, not castration (cf. Matthew 5:29, 30). There are those in the Kingdom who forgo marriage and the benefit of family in order to serve the Kingdom more effectively. Both John the Baptist and Jesus fit this category, but it is clear that Jesus expects such a course of action to be possible only for those who have been divinely enabled. In other words, those who have been given the gift of celibacy are encouraged to use it for the Kingdom's sake.

Implications for the Pentecostal Family

1. *Joseph's role as legal ancestor, protector, spiritual role model, and vocational teacher was essential for Jesus' own growth and development.* In many ways Joseph could be identified as an ideal father. His function and role emphasize for us the strategic work parents have, for no parent understands fully the precious gifts with which he/she has been entrusted.

2. *Jesus' family life appears to have been relatively normal.* This normality is demonstrated among other things by the tension of His brothers' unbelief. Clearly, Jesus possessed firsthand knowledge about the division of family that the Kingdom could bring. This experience means that Jesus can empathize with those who have unconverted family members.

3. *Jesus' family experience may even have included the shouldering of some parental responsibilities.* Evidently, Joseph died between Jesus' 12th year and the beginning of His public ministry. If such is the case, Jesus would have assumed responsibilities as head of the household. Because of the role assigned to women in first-century Palestine, both His mother and sisters would have needed the guardianship of a man. Not only did He care for His mother until His death and give charge of her to the Beloved Disciple (John 19:26, 27), but apparently He was also guardian for His sisters until the time of their marriage. Anyone who has struggled with the responsibilities of parenting can find comfort in the suggestion that Jesus may have faced such difficulties Himself.

4. *Jesus affirmed the honor due parents, and He defended their right to receive support and respect.* Not only did He affirm this principle, but He also

lived out such belief in His own life. Jesus cared for His mother until the Crucifixion; and it is also likely that when Joseph died, He oversaw His father's burial. Such a model of care and compassion is in sharp contrast to the treatment some parents and elderly receive in contemporary society, where many are assigned a place in the backwaters of existence, with little or no respect.

5. *Jesus' attitude toward children exalted their place in society and legitimized ministry to them.* If the Lord of Glory had time for children and appreciated their importance, who can claim to be too busy to find time for ministry with children?

6. *Jesus' attitude toward marriage was positive.* Not only did He honor it with His presence, but He also opposed divorce, and used marriage analogously for His teaching about the Kingdom. Jesus believed that most individuals would marry, for not everyone would be able to receive His teaching about eunuchs for the Kingdom. Such a high view of marriage implies divine sanction and approval. It also cautions those who treat divorce in a light or flippant fashion.

7. *A number of passages indicate that Jesus believed the call of God took priority over any other commitment.* It is clear that some in the early church had forsaken even family relationships for the Kingdom. One obvious example of such action is the apostle Peter, who left all to follow Jesus. There are hints, however, that he did not abandon his family. Mark 1:29-31 indicates that Peter and Andrew maintained a house where Peter's mother-in-law resided, while 1 Corinthians 9:5 implies that later in life Peter's wife traveled with him.

Pentecostal history is filled with accounts of those who have left family for extended periods of time to serve the Lord in a radical fashion. While many have legitimately fulfilled these words of Jesus, it must be admitted that His words have also been prostituted to serve less than holy agendas.

How can one discern if the Lord is leading to such a radical position? Honesty is absolutely essential in discovering the answer. While other elements are involved, one issue must be faced squarely. What is the motive for a specific course of action? If there is no one else who can serve the same function, if there is an extreme sense of urgency and the body of Christ confirms the move, then perhaps the Spirit is leading in that direction. However, if such absence from family is because of career building, political maneuvering, or the praise of others, then one may be in danger of violating those commands which the Lord himself affirmed. Perhaps a family covenant might prove most beneficial in balancing one's various responsibilities.

8. *It is clear from Jesus' teaching that He saw an extended family for the believer.* For those who had lost family relationships because of the Kingdom, a wealth of family would be inherited in this life. Of course with such benefits come great responsibilities. It may be that one of the real failures of the church is the neglect of the extended Christian family.

9. *Jesus affirmed the right of those who have been endowed with the ability to remain celibate.* Instead of denigrating the role of the single, the church should respect such individuals, make every effort to maximize their gifts, and ensure that their position within the extended Christian family is secure and honored.

UNITY AND DIVERSITY: OBSTACLE OR OPPORTUNITY?

For a movement facing the challenges that await the Church of God, few topics are more relevant than "Leadership and Conflict." This chapter seeks to identify some of the ways in which the issues of diversity and unity relate to conflict. After a brief introduction, specific texts from the Book of Acts will be examined in an attempt to discern a biblical model for addressing the issues of diversity and unity.

Decisions concerning internationalization, racial issues, social action, and the role of women in the church and ministry all involve, in one way or another, the delicate balance between unity and diversity. Needless to say, there is no unanimity of thought in our movement on any one of these issues, let alone consensus on all of them. How, then, can the church, whose leadership and decision makers are predominantly male, white, and North American, hope to address such complex issues, all of which bear directly on the church's purpose and mission? Such challenges must be faced squarely, lest diversity result in everyone doing what is right in one's own eyes, or lest uniformity be misinterpreted as unity.

From the onset it should be noted that there is an essential unity in the writings which make up the New Testament and among the writers and communities that lie behind these documents. Such unity may be briefly identified as belief in (1) Jesus Christ as the living and resurrected Messiah, who is the Son of God, (2) His atoning death for the sins of humanity, (3) the empowering work of the Holy Spirit for the church and individual believers, (4) the return of Jesus to earth, (5) one God, (6) the Hebrew Scriptures, and others. The unity of the early church may be seen in its corporate worship, the one loaf and cup from which the body partook, as well as its one baptism.

At the same time, there is New Testament evidence of diversity of thought over an abundance of issues, ranging from attitudes regarding the significance of the Temple to views about the legitimacy of admitting Gentiles into the church. Dietary laws, circumcision, feast days, and a host of other issues were all very much in dispute in a number of first-century churches. Such diversity destroys the myth that the early church was a monolithic group where everyone thought and acted identically.

Instead of leaving us discouraged, this aspect of the biblical text should encourage us in that the early church faced issues no less complicated than those which currently face the Church of God. Given the nature of our challenges and the authority of the biblical text, select passages in the Book of Acts are now examined.

Unity and Diversity in the Book of Acts

Although this theme has been long overlooked by mainstream scholarship, there is a consensus emerging among Pentecostal/Charismatic Lukan scholars that one of Luke's primary purposes in the Book of Acts was to emphasize the way in which various groups within the church are charismatically anointed for service.[1]

In addition to Luke's concern to document the expansion or growth of the church, he had a special desire to demonstrate the way the Holy Spirit was given for empowerment for witness, regardless of gender, race, nationality, or religious background. To accomplish his goal Luke often introduced, in a very subtle fashion, themes that will later be given more dedicated attention.

The contents of the first five chapters of Acts hardly need to be rehearsed for Pentecostal readers. The outpouring of the Holy Spirit on the Day of Pentecost, inspired witness, healings, miraculous

---

[1]Cf. especially, Roger Stronstad, *The Charismatic Theology of St. Luke* (Peabody: Hendrickson, 1984); French Arrington, *The Acts of the Apostles* (Peabody: Hendrickson, 1988); Robert Menzies, *Empowered for Witness: The Spirit in Luke-Acts* (JPTS 6; Sheffield: Sheffield Academic Press, 1994); and James Shelton, *Mighty in Word and Deed* (Peabody: Hendrickson, 1991).

signs, and persecution are all found here. Chapter 5 ends with the apostles, in open defiance of the Jerusalem religious leaders, continually teaching and preaching Jesus in the Temple.

The first section of Acts 6 is well known for its importance in the discussion about church offices. The term *diakonos* occurs at this point in the Greek text. Acts 6 is also well known in Pentecostal circles because these "servants" were all full of the Holy Spirit, Stephen being the prime example. Another dimension of the text, however, is important for the present discussion. At this point Luke first reveals diversity in the earliest church. Here he introduced two distinct groups within the church, the Hellenists and the *Hebraioi.*[2]

Luke seems to be doing a couple of things in mentioning these two groups at this time. The words of Jesus in Acts 1:8 reveal that the disciples were to be witnesses in Jerusalem, Judea, Samaria, and the extreme portions of the earth. Up to this point, the witness of the early church had been focused on Jerusalem. Luke appears to use this episode to make the transition from Jerusalem to Judea, Samaria, Rome, and beyond.[3] For it was through the efforts of Philip, one of the seven Hellenists, the gospel was

---

[2]In this chapter, the term *Hebraioi* has simply been transliterated from the Greek text, because most English translations obscure its meaning. In the following discussion, the meaning of the term will become clear.

[3]There is now firm philological evidence that the phrase "to the ends of the earth" (ἕως ἐσξάτον τῆς γῆς) has reference generally to Spain and more specifically the city of Gades. Cf. E. Earle Ellis, "The Ends of the Earth: Acts 1:8," *Bulletin for Biblical Research* 1 (1991), pp. 123-32. For Luke to mention "the ends of the earth" but then to leave Paul and the reader in Rome suggests that Acts 28 is not the end of the story but accomplishes Luke's purpose.

initially preached in Samaria (8:4-13) and Judea (8:26-40) and for the first time to a Gentile (the Ethiopian eunuch).[4] Through the persecution of the Hellenists, the first real mission to the Gentiles began (11:19-30) and the issue of the Gentile mission was eventually addressed in Jerusalem. In addition, through the ministry of one of the ministers to the Hellenists, Saul, the gospel reached Rome.[5]

At the same time Luke was making this transition in the narrative, he also introduced the idea of diversity in the early church. The appearance of the Hellenists and the Hebraioi in Acts 6:1 takes the reader completely by surprise, for there has been no hint, up to this point, that any such diversity existed. However one defines these two groups, one thing is clear: a conflict had arisen in the early church over unequal support of the Hellenistic widows. In order to understand the precise nature of this conflict, these two groups must be more clearly identified.

The Hellenists and the Hebraioi

Initially, one might be tempted to identify the Hellenists as Gentiles and the Hebraioi as Jews, but to this point in the Acts narrative, everyone in the early church was Jewish. One could hardly expect the discussions which the Cornelius event and the mission to the Gentiles would later evoke if indeed there were already Gentiles in the community. In fact,

---

[4]Cf. especially the suggestion of Michel Quesnel [*Baptises dans l' Esprit* (Paris: Cerf, 1985), p. 33 n. 5] that in Acts the conversion of the Gentiles is described in three steps: a preparation (Acts 8:26-40), a central event (Acts 10:1-11, 18), and an extension (Acts 11:19-26).

[5]For Paul's ministry to the Hellenists cf. Acts 9:29 and 11:19-26.

Luke made clear that both the Hellenists and the Hebraioi were Christians, using the term *disciple* (μαθητής) here for the first time—and they were Jewish Christians at that.[6] What distinction, then, did Luke wish to draw between these two groups?

It is possible to describe these groups along linguistic lines: Hellenists spoke Greek, the Hebraioi spoke Hebrew. However, the explanation is not quite that simple. For example, Paul referred to himself as a Hebrew of Hebrews (Philippians 3:5), but he wrote in Greek, even showing a decided preference for the Septuagint (the Greek translation of the Old Testament), a preference not all New Testament writers shared. Additionally, the letter to the Hebrews is written in some of the best Greek found in the New Testament. It would seem, then, that the intended distinction between these groups is more than that of language.

Neither should the Hebraioi be taken as those Jews who lived in Palestine nor the Hellenists to refer to those who were from the Diaspora. Synagogues of the Hebraioi have been found as far away from Palestine as Rome, while Jerusalem itself showed abundant signs of Hellenization. After all, the highest Jewish court in the land had a Greek name, the Sanhedrin.[7]

Rather, it appears that Luke intended to make theological distinctions between these two groups. Based

---

[6]Given the fact that Luke had a perfectly good word to use for Gentile ('Ελληνικός) but did not is also evidence that in making reference to the Hellenists, Luke has a particular group of Jewish Christians in mind.

[7]Martin Hengel [*Between Jesus and Paul* (Philadelphia: Fortress, 1983), p. 7] concludes, "The archeological evidence for the period before 70 shows that Jewish Galilee was not more but less Hellenized than Jerusalem."

on hints in Stephen's speech, the ensuing persecution of the Christian Hellenists, and the nature of their mission to the Gentiles, it is possible to reconstruct some of their attitudes and beliefs.[8]

Not long after being named as a minister (διάκονος), Stephen encountered opposition from the Synagogue of the Freedman—Jews from Cyrene, Alexandria, Cilicia, and Asia. These false witnesses charged, "This fellow never stops speaking against the holy place and against the law. For we have heard him say that this Jesus of Nazareth will destroy this place and change the customs Moses handed down to us" (Acts 6:13, 14, *NIV*).

Although it is clear that the witnesses who testified against Stephen were false, the basis of their accusations becomes evident from Stephen's speech in Acts 7. While careful to emphasize the place of the Tabernacle in Israel's history, Stephen did not extend this positive assessment to the Temple. The Tabernacle was designed by God himself, Stephen said, but Solomon built "the house" for Him (God). "However (ἀλλ'), the Most High does not live in houses made by men" (Acts 7:48). For Stephen the Temple had lost its significance with the coming of the Messiah.

Stephen's activity and death prompted a severe persecution of the believers. In particular, the persecution was directed against the Hellenist Christians. As was noted earlier, it was through this group that the words of Jesus in Acts 1:8 were fulfilled. Oddly, the

---

[8]I would like to thank Dr. William Simmons of Lee College for an extremely insightful and vigorous dialogue regarding the Hellenists. For a detailed discussion of the Hellenists and their role in the early church cf. William Simmons, *Jesus and Paul: A Theology of Inclusion* (New York: Mellen Biblical Press, 1996).

apostles were not affected. Could it be that the apostles and those of like mind were not subjected to this persecution because they did not challenge the validity of the Temple?

Stephen's perspective was not an isolated view in the early church. This is confirmed by evidence found in the Book of Hebrews. Here, the author's premise is that since Jesus has come, the Temple and its cultus are no longer a necessary part of worship. Jesus, the reality to whom these shadows pointed, has made their use obsolete. The whole point is that sacrifices and Temple worship are no longer valid. Such an emphasis is not only evidence for a liberal attitude toward Temple and Torah on the part of some early Christians, but it also indicates that there were Jewish Christians for whom the Temple and its system held a great deal of attraction.

Luke appears to use two terms to describe those Jewish Christians who were more conservative in their attitudes to Temple and Torah: the *Hebraioi* and "those of the circumcision" (see Acts 10:45). Acts 6 suggests that the Hebraioi are contrasted with the Hellenists in some ways. If this analysis of the Hellenists is accurate, the Hebraioi were no doubt in some ways more conservative than the Hellenists. It appears that the Hebraioi are to be identified with "those of the circumcision." It is clear that in the Book of Acts "those of the circumcision" formed a distinct group in the early church, for after Cornelius' Spirit baptism, Peter was confronted by this group in the Jerusalem church (Acts 11:2).

Since all the Christians in Jerusalem at this time were Jewish, and observed circumcision, the use of the phrase "those of the circumcision" must convey a message regarding their theological orientation. Thus, it appears that the Hebraioi and "those of the circumcision" are designations used for Jewish Christians who were more conservative with regard to Temple, Torah, and daily living than were their Hellenist brothers and sisters. In contrast to the Hellenists, these believers were convinced that the most appropriate means by which to live out the life of a believer was in accordance with the Torah and the Temple. While the coming of the Messiah had great implications for these individuals, it did not follow for them that the Temple should be abandoned nor the Torah radically reinterpreted.

The role of the Temple for the early church and particularly for this group is documented by Luke. He ended his Gospel (24:53) with an account that the followers of Jesus were always in the Temple. The Day of Pentecost documents the close proximity of the believers to the Temple. Not long afterward, Peter and John were instrumental in the healing of a lame man at the Temple gate (Acts 3:1-10). On another occasion Peter received divine instruction to preach in the Temple courts (5:20), and some of the believers often taught in the Temple (v. 42). Years later certain Jerusalem Christians informed Paul that thousands of Jews believed in Jesus and were zealous for the law (Acts 21:20). On this occasion Paul was warned that he stood accused of forsaking the teaching of Moses and seeking to abolish its propagation. These passages demonstrate that while the Temple was a natural meeting place for some in early Christianity, the Hebraioi seem to have been tied very closely to the Temple as a religious symbol and were not prepared to give it up despite the coming of Jesus.

Acts 6:1-7

With this understanding of the Hellenists and the Hebraioi, this passage (Acts 6:1-7) may be explored more closely:

> In those days when the number of disciples was increasing, the Hellenists among them complained against the Hebraioi because their widows were being overlooked in the daily distribution of food. So the Twelve gathered all the disciples together and said, "It would not be right for us to neglect the ministry of the word of God in order to wait on tables. Brothers, choose seven men from among you who are known to be full of the Spirit and wisdom. We will turn this responsibility over to them and will give our attention to prayer and the ministry of the word." This proposal pleased the whole group. They chose Stephen, a man full of faith and of the Holy Spirit; also Philip, Procorus, Nicanor, Timon, Parmenas, and Nicolas from Antioch, a convert [προσήλυτον] to Judaism. They presented these men to the apostles, who prayed and laid their hands on them.
>
> So the word of God spread. The number of disciples in Jerusalem increased rapidly, and a large number of priests became obedient to the faith (*NIV*).

It is clear from this text that a conflict had arisen over the support of the Hellenist widows. The grievance was either taken to the apostles or it made its way quickly to them. Whether the Twelve were themselves involved in the distribution of food or not, as leaders of the community they were ultimately responsible. Rather than attempt to handle this conflict in secret, the Twelve brought it to the attention of all the believers. Explaining the situation and acknowledging their own primary obligations to the Word of God (Luke may have used "the Twelve" here to emphasize their role as those set apart for the proclamation of the gospel [cf. Luke 9:1-9; Acts 1:26; 2:14]), the apostles instructed the church to choose seven individuals to whom they could entrust the responsibility of ministering to the needs of the widows.

What happened next was truly amazing. Despite any misgivings that the believers (the majority of which were no doubt Hebraioi) might have had regarding the "liberal" tendencies of their Hellenist brothers and sisters, they selected seven individuals, all of whom had Greek names.[9] There was even one proselyte in this group. Faced with one of its first conflicts, the church demonstrated extraordinary courage and trust. If there were problems with the way the Hellenist widows were being cared for, the church would ensure adequate care by appointing Hellenists to oversee the care of all widows, including the Hebraioi. Rather than clinging to the power that such oversight would bring, the Hebraioi responded by renouncing all such claims in order that their Hellenist brothers and sisters would be assured of proper care.

The wisdom of the church's decision is evidenced in two ways. First, the Word of God spread—in part, no doubt, because the Twelve were able to devote full attention to prayer and the ministry of the Word. Luke's mention that a number of priests had come to faith may indicate that the focus of the Twelve's ministry was the Hebraioi, individuals with whom they would share certain attitudes toward the Temple and the Torah.

---

[9]Arrington, *The Acts of the Apostles*, p. 66

Second, by placing their own concerns below those of their Hellenist brothers and sisters, the church in effect unleashed the very individuals whom God would use to take the gospel beyond the borders of Jerusalem. One would have expected the Twelve to be at the heart of this missionary enterprise, and they no doubt had their place. But Luke chose to highlight another stream in the early church, one in which the Hellenists were crucial. The irony is that by commissioning the Hellenists, an unbelievable missionary force was unleashed by those very people who had been commissioned by Jesus himself for such a task.

Of course this decision was not the only one the church would have to make as the result of conflict, as Peter's later experience and that of the Jerusalem Council demonstrate. One quickly led to another in a way that the Jerusalem church could hardly have foreseen. Yet the church faced each conflict in a way that sought to bring the church together, to listen to the Spirit, to hear the testimonies of those involved, and to consult the Scriptures.[10]

Consistently, those in leadership were not afraid of empowering those with whom they had little contact—or control, for that matter—in order to discern the will of God in each situation. While the Hebraioi continued to go to the Temple and paid careful attention to various dimensions of the Torah, they also acknowledged

---

[10]Cf. the helpful discussion by French Arrington, "Hermeneutics," *Dictionary of the Pentecostal and Charismatic Movements*, eds. S. Burgess and G. McGee (Grand Rapids: Zondervan, 1988), pp. 387-388. Cf. also J.C. Thomas, "Women, Pentecostals, and the Bible: An Experiment in Pentecostal Hermeneutics," *Journal of Pentecostal Theology* 5 (1994), pp. 41-56.

and commissioned those who understood such elements as having been made null and void by the coming of the Messiah.

Would the church have fulfilled its mission as described in Acts if it had not entrusted one of its ministries to a group of Hellenists? It is hard to answer such a question, but no doubt the heart of God would have been grieved in the process.

Conclusions and Implications

Reflecting on that question should lead us naturally to consider some of the challenges currently facing the Church of God. Each challenge represents conflict in one form or another, but each is crucial to the mission of the church.

Is it possible that in the issues of internationalization, racism, social justice, and the role of women in the church and its ministry God is challenging the church to commission and unleash whole missionary movements?

Could it be that by taking radical actions like the early church did, we would not only ensure a place for the various constituencies but also witness the return of the Lord because of such missionary empowerment?

What if the church sought out Holy Spirit-filled internationals, blacks, Hispanics, women, and those who fight for social justice to lead the whole church as we seek to live out the kingdom of God on earth? Would we not learn? Would we not be that much closer to the Kingdom? Would the Father not be pleased and the Holy Spirit be manifested in ways we have not had the faith to envision?

Of course there are Judaizers and antinomians in our movement, just as there were in the early church, who seek to control the work of God through legalism and lawlessness. But the presence of those who outdistance the gospel in such ways should not deter us from following the Spirit in the issues that face us any more than counterfeit gifts keep us from seeking the manifestation of the Spirit in our worship.

I would humbly submit that it is time for us to forsake business as usual in the church—whether at the local, state, or general levels—and take the kinds of actions that will result in the unleashing of all our resources for the mission of the church. Each of us must respond to this challenge, for the stakes are too high. Rabbi Akiba is quoted as asking, "If not me, who? If not now, when?"

THE JESUS SEMINAR: A CRITICAL EXAMINATION OF JESUS' WORDS AND WORKS

In 1985 a group of New Testament scholars began to assess, in a critical fashion, the life and words of Jesus. They released their initial findings in early 1991. The results of the seminar's work caused quite a stir among Christians of all denominations.

This chapter is an assessment of the seminar's work from a Pentecostal viewpoint, and a response to it. To become acquainted with the many significant dimensions of this issue, the following aspects must be included:

- A description of the nature and purpose of the Jesus Seminar's work
- An assessment of the basic assumptions of the seminar

- A critique of the seminar's results
- The implications of this material

The Nature and Purpose of the Seminar

The seminar was created by Robert Funk, a retired professor of religious studies, who established the Westar Institute, an academic think tank in Sonoma, California. The composition of the seminar's participants included scholars from most mainline church denominations and representatives from many seminaries and universities. Only two of the members represented conservative positions.

The primary work of the seminar was to examine 503 recorded sayings of Jesus. After an extensive analysis of an individual saying, every member of the group expressed his/her opinion about whether the words were actually uttered by Jesus. The voting was conducted using colored beads, each of four colors signifying a particular decision about the authenticity or trustworthiness of the saying. A red bead signified that the saying goes back to Jesus. A pink bead suggested that Jesus said something similar to the recorded saying. A gray bead stood for ideas close to Jesus' ideas. A black bead meant the saying was wholly the work of the early church, not the work of Jesus. Each colored bead was given a value so that the votes could be averaged.

One of the goals of this seminar was to make the conclusions available to the general public. Participants sought to offer an alternative to television ministers who claim a special authority to interpret the Bible. The seminar was organized to enlighten the masses with "the truth" about Jesus.

Basic Assumptions of the Jesus Seminar

Instead of approaching the Gospels as inspired and trustworthy texts that possess an inherent authority, most seminar members treated the Gospels simply as religious literature which may contain some information that actually goes back to Jesus. One of their basic assumptions was that while there may be genuine sayings of Jesus in the Gospels, it is difficult to identify them or to be certain of their trustworthiness. This problem exists, they contended, because the early church modified the teaching of Jesus through its teaching and preaching. Therefore it is not clear if one is dealing with the words of Jesus or the thought and teaching of the early church in any Gospel passage.

Simply put, most seminar members believed the Gospels mirrored the early church's life and theological reflection, which may or may not be based on Jesus' own teaching. They contended that one must carefully sift the words and thoughts of Jesus from that of primitive Christianity.

To distinguish between the authentic words of Jesus and those sayings the Gospel writers—and/or the early church—attributed to Jesus, scholars have devised certain tests or criteria, often called the criteria of authenticity. These tests are intended to allow one to identify those sayings of Jesus that most certainly owe their origin to Him. Ordinarily, four criteria are used with the most emphasis being placed upon the first one.

Criterion of Dissimilarity. This test, as its name implies, seeks to identify sayings of Jesus that are dissimilar or unique. The criterion has three parts:

First, if a saying displays the ideas and concerns of

the early church, it is assumed that the saying owes its origin to the early church, not to Jesus.

Second, if a saying is such that any of Jesus' Jewish contemporaries could have said it, then it is assumed that the saying is a piece of popular teaching that has been attributed to Jesus.

Third, if the saying exhibits neither of these characteristics, it can be assumed that Jesus actually uttered these words.

Criterion of Multiple Attestation. This criterion assumes that the more often a saying, theme, or event appears in different portions of the New Testament besides parallel accounts, the more likely it is that the material goes back to Jesus.

Criterion of Linguistic and Cultural Tests. This criterion assumes that the more Semitic (Aramaic) or Palestinian a saying is in character, the less likely it is the material originated in the Hellenistic church.

Criterion of Coherence. This criterion attributes to Jesus material that would not be accepted on its own but is similar to sayings proven by one or more of the other criteria used.

These tests are very important to a number of biblical scholars, including many members of the Jesus Seminar. Without an acquaintance with these criteria, it is virtually impossible to understand the work of the seminar.

An Assessment of the Seminar's Assumptions

One of the most obvious assumptions many seminar members had was that one cannot presume that the Gospel materials go back to Jesus but, rather, that each saying must be proven to go back to Him. This is no isolated assumption. Many hold that the burden of proof lies with those who believe that Jesus' sayings are authentic. Therefore, many share a deep suspicion about the trustworthiness of His sayings in general. But is such a negative starting point justified? The answer is no, for a number of reasons.

1. In such historical skepticism the role of eyewitnesses is completely ignored. To omit this vital factor from consideration produces an extremely distorted view of the material's trustworthiness. In fact, the eyewitnesses of Jesus' ministry and Resurrection figured significantly in the life and structure of the early church. Not only did they serve as leaders, but they would no doubt also have helped to preserve the Gospel materials from distortion. It is simply too difficult to believe that the eyewitnesses of Jesus' life and teaching would not have an interest in or a desire to collect the sayings of Jesus and preserve them from wholesale modification.

This point deserves a hearing even if the eyewitnesses had nothing to do with the composition of the Gospels. But instead of eyewitnesses playing no role in the writing of the Gospel accounts, all four documents rely directly or indirectly on eyewitnesses and, in several cases, apostolic testimony.

2. Another flaw is the assumption that the primitive church did not try to distinguish Jesus' words from its own. This position is inaccurate on several counts:

First, the very fact that several Gospels were written demonstrates an interest in the life and words of Jesus. If any of the evangelists had merely been interested in theology, they could have written epistles or other works.

Second, the Pauline Epistles carefully distinguish the words of Jesus from Paul's own. First Corinthians 7:8-12 is an example of how such clear distinctions were made.

Third, the early church took great pains to differentiate between the words of Jesus during His earthly ministry and His words which were given in post-Resurrection visions (Revelation 1:9-20).

Finally, many (liberal and conservative) scholars believe that some of the first materials written down were Jesus' sayings. If such collections existed, and surely they did, it is unlikely that the lines between Jesus' words and those of the early church would be blurred.

3. Another false assumption was that since the Gospel materials were passed on orally before they were written down, numerous modifications were made which undermine the integrity of the material. Yet, this scenario ignores several vital pieces of evidence.

It is possible that one or more of the disciples made notes on the central teaching of Jesus during His earthly ministry. Matthew, in particular, is a prime candidate for such a task, due to his scribal activities. In addition, if Matthew is to be identified with Levi, then he would be aware of the value of Jesus' teaching in the light of the previous sacred history of Israel in the Old Testament.

It is also probable that some of Jesus' teachings would be written down in different locations after He left that particular area. Such records of His sayings would serve as teaching resources in the absence of Jesus and His disciples.

In like fashion, it is most probable that before going out to preach, the disciples either committed to memory or wrote down certain portions of Jesus' message. Even the proposal that Jesus' teaching was passed on orally does not imply a haphazard transmission of the materials. Memorization was a vital tool for preserving materials of various kinds. The advent of economical and readily available resources for recording materials has eroded this skill for many. In many cultures, however, traditional materials are still passed on with little modification through this method of transmission. To assume that the sayings of Jesus were modified in an unrestricted fashion falls more into the realm of hypothesis than the realm of fact.

Finally, an assessment must be offered of the criteria of authenticity. This critique is based on the first criterion alone (dissimilarity) due to its strategic nature. In fact, many scholars will accept the results of this test only. Therefore, attention must be focused here.

If one uses this test, a few sayings of Jesus can be identified as authentic. The problem with this is that the sayings are not very valuable. On the one hand, since only the sayings acknowledged as authentic are those distinct from what other Jews of the first century may have said, much of what Jesus assumed and shared with his environment is not considered. This approach results in an artificial view of Jesus. On the other hand, since the sayings of Jesus which were prominent in the teaching of the early church are disallowed, the result is sayings in which the church did not show a great deal of interest. In short, this criterion may produce some sayings, but they are peripheral at best and produce an inaccurate picture of Jesus.

A Critique of the Seminar's Results

Two conclusions of the seminar merit specific attention, for they challenge basic and essential points of Christian faith.

It was decided by the Seminar that Jesus did not say the Lord's Prayer. At best, the prayer reflects little of Jesus' own words except the addressing of God as Father. In addition to the general response to such historical skepticism offered earlier, three additional points may be made here:

1. Jesus' addressing God as Father is consistent with His words in many other places in the Gospels. This form of address is one of the things which distinguishes Jesus from other Jews in the first century.

2. In contrast to other first-century Jewish prayers, the Lord's Prayer is very concise and structured.

3. If the early church produced this prayer instead of Jesus, one would expect to find reference to issues of importance for primitive Christianity, such as spiritual gifts, the Gentile mission, religious and political persecution. Such late concerns are missing from the prayer, however.

The Jesus Seminar concluded that Jesus never taught that He would come again. Most seminar members held that Jesus taught the kingdom of God is a present reality, or that the Kingdom would come in the future. In the seminar's view, Jesus could not have held to both emphases. Consequently, many of them believed that Jesus was concerned with the Kingdom as a present phenomenon, not a future one. However, such a conclusion overlooks the following pieces of evidence:

1. The teaching about Jesus' return is in some of the

earliest Christian literature (1 and 2 Thessalonians). This fact suggests that there was never a time when the church did not believe in this teaching.

2. One of the earliest Christian greetings was "Maranatha" (1 Corinthians 16:22), which emphasizes the Lord's return. What makes this term all the more impressive is that *maranatha* is an Aramaic word which is not translated into Greek but is transliterated into Greek. This evidence points out that while the church was in Palestine, belief in the Lord's return was accepted.

3. The tension between present and future dimensions of the Kingdom may be hard for contemporary scholars to accept, but most Jewish Christians were comfortable with holding various ideas together which were equally as difficult—for example, predestination and free will, as well as the oneness of God and the deity of Jesus.

4. In perhaps the first Gospel written, there is an extended discourse about Jesus' return (Mark 13). This material, which exhibits signs of being quite old, demonstrates that the return of Jesus was part of the Gospel proclamation from the beginning.

Implications and Conclusions

Perhaps the most important aspect of the Jesus Seminar was the stated purpose of the scholars involved to make their conclusions known to the public. Positions held by many seminar members are no different from that of many liberal scholars, but the seminar seeks to publicize its views. This brings these opinions out of the classroom into full view by the public, which means that a much wider audience will be exposed to them.

The seminar's work could complicate the work of the church in two ways:

First, the seminar's opinions may cause some believers to question and/or doubt the reliability of the New Testament and, in turn, question their belief in the Lord.

Second, these conclusions will be an additional obstacle for some unbelievers who might otherwise come to faith.

The days of the cliché "God said it, I believe it, that settles it" may soon be over. The response of the church to the charges of such scholars requires careful study and much reflection. Therefore, the church must give specific attention to two areas.

First, pastors and other Christian leaders must prepare themselves to address such questions when they are raised, within or outside the church. Most often, the pastor will be the person called upon for an opinion. His or her response may have a significant bearing on the individual questioners.

Second, Pentecostal schools must prepare their students to assess and critique these views. The day is past when such opinions could be written off without an examination. The Jesus Seminar is changing all of that. Defending the faith has never been more crucial or timely.

THE PRAYER OF FAITH IN JAMES 5:14-16

The relationship between the devil and disease,
sickness and sin, healing and forgiveness, and exorcism and deliverance is an intriguing issue. Biblical
scholars have long debated the exact understanding
of Christians, Jews, and pagans about such matters.
Pastoral psychologists, counselors, and social scien-
tists have made several attempts to integrate the psy-
chic, physiological, and the spiritual dimensions of
mental and physical health.

But scholarly interests pale in comparison to the
attention this topic receives at the popular level within the Pentecostal and Charismatic traditions. It seems
that Pentecostals and Charismatics can generally be
divided into the following three categories:

First, there are those who see lurking behind every illness or misfortune demonic activity. For these believers there is a clear line of demarcation between the devil (illness) and God (healing). In every circumstance the believer is to rebuke Satan, curse the demonic oppression, and utilize the authority God has bestowed upon him/her through Jesus Christ. Generally, those who take this position attribute any failure to receive healing to a deficiency on the part of those who pray. A lack of faith or the presence of sin might prevent healing, but it is never God's will for a believer to continue in such suffering. God's will is for all to be healed.

A second group within the tradition would maintain that while all disease is from the devil, not every individual sick person is ill as the direct result of satanic attack. While there are instances of believers suffering disease at the hands of Satan, many Christians may become sick from "natural causes." Such a position is advocated for a couple of reasons. First, many of these believers hold that since sin and sickness entered the world through the fall of Adam, and will not finally be removed until the Parousia (the return of Christ), individual Christians are just as likely to suffer physically as unbelievers. Such is the fate of those who live in a fallen world. Second, the idea that demons can possess and/or oppress Christians is viewed at best as resting on very meager biblical support, and at worst as an unbiblical heresy.

The bottom line is, these individuals believe that not every illness can be attributed directly to the devil. Implied in this assessment is that God might sometimes use suffering for His glory. Prayer for the sick is always legitimate, but it might not always be God's will to bring physical healing. *A final group is comprised of what might be called "functional deists."* These believers genuinely believe in God's power to heal and the devil's ability to inflict suffering, but have become rather disengaged and detached from the whole business. On the one hand, this apathy is, in part, the result of outlandish and sometimes embarrassing claims made by some proponents of divine healing. When healing does not occur, these individuals are faced with the dilemma of seeking to reconcile this failure to receive healing with claims that it is always God's will to heal.

On the other hand, many believers are so frustrated by the inability to know whether it is God's will to heal in a specific situation that they choose simply to become onlookers rather than participants. It would be wrong to assume that such individuals never pray for healing; but if and when healings occur, these believers are ordinarily astounded by the results. At the very least, such individuals bring a somewhat skeptical attitude to the enterprise and do not usually offer fervent prayers for healing. No doubt many of us fit into one of these three categories. (Some may have even shifted from one group to another—more than once!)

As one who serves in the seminary and in the parish, I am both troubled and perplexed by the current attitudes toward sickness and divine healing. Two aspects are most disconcerting: First, the confusion over the relationship between sin and sickness has caused many of our brothers and sisters to be less certain about God's ability and desire to intervene in this world to bring healing. Such uncertainty serves to undermine one of the five foundational beliefs which characterized early Pentecostalism.[1] Second, such confusion regarding divine healing suggests that biblical scholars working within the tradition have not done their homework on this topic, at least in a form that is readily accessible. Therefore, I propose that we embark on an exegetical and interpretive journey to discover what the Bible says about the devil, disease, and deliverance. Such an ambitious sojourn is certainly too long to complete in this short chapter, but perhaps the first tentative steps may be taken.

With so much terrain to cover, one might legitimately ask, Why begin with James 5? Several reasons may be offered in support of this decision:

1. James 5:14-16 gives us a glimpse into how one early Christian church ministered to believers who were suffering physically. Of the many New Testament passages which advocate divine healing, this is the only text that describes a procedure to be followed.

2. This passage makes explicit the fact that sin and sickness are sometimes related.

3. James appears to assume that healing from physical infirmities is an expected and ongoing part of the community's life.

4. The church represented by the Epistle of James appears to be distinctively non-Pauline in theological perspective and focus. It may be helpful, therefore, to begin this journey with a less prominent form of early Christian thought in order to appreciate more fully

---

[1]Steven J. Land has shown that the early Pentecostal view of Jesus included five primary dimensions: Jesus as Savior, Sanctifier, Holy Ghost Baptizer, Healer, and Coming King. See S.J. Land, *Pentecostal Spirituality: A Passion for the Kingdom* (JPTS Series 1; Sheffield, England: Sheffield Academic Press, 1993).

the diversity which is to be found in the early church and to gain leverage on this complex topic.

5. A final reason for choosing James 5 as the first point of inquiry is related to the importance of this text in Pentecostal life and practice. In *Theological Roots of Pentecostalism*, Donald Dayton shows that the rise of the divine healing movement is an indispensable backdrop for viewing the emergence of Pentecostalism.[2] By the end of the 19th century, healing ministries were quite common.[3] Understandably, James 5:14-16 became one of the more significant texts for this doctrine and practice.[4] The relationship between sin and sickness, suggested in James 5:14-16, raised many questions and caused disagreement and division among advocates and antagonists alike.[5] Therefore a reexamination of James 5:14-16 seems most appropriate.

The remainder of this chapter consists of an exegetical analysis of James 5:14-16, a summary of tentative conclusions on the topic, and a projection for future research on this issue.

A few things are assumed about the Epistle of James in this study. It appears to come from a Jewish-Christian milieu and from a primitive community. The attention to grace and works notwithstanding, it is not

---

[2] D.W. Dayton, *Theological Roots of Pentecostalism* (Grand Rapids: Zondervan, 1987), pp. 115-141.

[3] See P.G. Chappell, "Healing Movements," *Dictionary of Pentecostal and Charismatic Movements*, eds. S.M. Burgess and G.B. McGee (Grand Rapids: Zondervan, 1988), pp. 353-374.

[4] Dayton, pp. 124-125.

[5] Compare the attitude of C. Cullis (*Faith Cures; or, Answers to Prayer in the Healing of the Sick* [Boston: Willard Tract Repository, 1879]), an early proponent of divine healing, with that of W.P. Harrison ("Faithcure in the Light of Scripture," *Methodist Quarterly Review*, 28 [1889] pp. 402-405), an early critic of divine healing.

altogether certain that James was composed in reaction to the Pauline mission. Indeed, one would expect much more attention to be given to issues such as circumcision if James were written as a polemic against Paul. It appears that James is a document which preserves testimony regarding early Christian practice that emerged in isolation from the Pauline mission.

An Examination of James 5:14-16

This passage occurs near the end of the epistle in a context which delineates appropriate responses to various situations in life. After directing those in trouble to pray and those who are happy to sing praises to God, James turned his attention to those in the community who were sick.

Verse 14

Are there any sick among you? An overwhelming majority of scholars understand James to have been addressing those who are physically sick with his use of the term translated "sick" (ἀσθενέω). Only a handful of writers maintain that James was referring to those who are emotionally or spiritually discouraged. That the Greek word for *sick* (ἀσθενέω) here refers to physical illness is borne out by several facts:

First, this term ἀσθενέω and its related words "are the most common NT expressions for sickness."[6]

Second, the Greek word for *trouble* (κακοπαθέω) in verse 13 almost certainly refers to personal distress produced by physical circumstances or personal situa-

---

[6]G. Stahlin, "ἀσθενής," *Theological Dictionary of the New Testament*, Vol. I, (ed. G. Kittel; trans. G.W. Bromiley; Grand Rapids: Eerdmans, 1964), p. 492.

tions other than sickness. The appearance of the term sick (ἀσθενέω) on the heels of trouble (κακοπαθέω) would suggest a change of topic, from those who are distressed or discouraged to those who are physically sick. In the light of such evidence it seems that James was addressing those in the community who were physically ill.

Call for the elders of the church. In contrast to his instructions in verse 13 for individual (and/or private) prayer, James admonished those who were sick to "call for the elders of the church." Such a directive may imply that the sick person was too ill to attend the community's corporate worship but had to request a visit to his or her home from the leaders of the church. However, such a conclusion may be a bit premature. For the term used here for "sick" does not necessarily imply a grave illness, and a number of places where "call" (προσκαλέω) occurs in the New Testament depict a summoning of individuals or groups in close proximity to the one who calls. Consequently, it is not clear whether the believer was to receive prayer from the elders in a context of public worship or at his or her home. What is clear is that the sick person was to call for prayer by the elders.

The appearance of groups of elders in the New Testament is remarkably widespread. They are mentioned in connection with the Jerusalem church (Acts 11:30; 15:2, 4, 6, 22, 23; 16:4; 21:18), the Pauline mission (Acts 14:23; 20:17-38), the Pauline circle (1 Timothy 4:14; 5:17-19; Titus 1:5), and the Petrine churches (1 Peter 5:1). In addition to these occurrences of *elder,* the author of 2 and 3 John refers to himself as "the elder." It may be concluded that the term *elder* designates a position of leadership in the early church, perhaps modeled after the practice of the synagogue.

As has often been noted, James did not advocate calling for those who possess the charisma, or gift, of healing, which would have been likely in the Pauline community (as 1 Corinthians 12 implies). Why did James not instruct the sick person to call for those in the community known to possess the gift of healing? Is James' directive a put-down of such claims? Or does this verse suggest that the charismata were unknown to James and/or his church? Several explanations have been offered to untie this mysterious knot.

One approach to the issue is to assume that leaders of the early local churches most certainly possessed the gift of healing. Does it not seem likely that individuals who possessed the gift of healing would naturally become leaders within their particular local Christian community? Such an understanding clearly assumes that James' community was familiar with the charismata and seeks to harmonize the experience of the Pauline communities with that of James.

Another approach is to connect the power to heal with the office of elder itself. This proposal has the advantage of being able to explain why the elders are called for without bringing the charismata into the discussion. It does, however, necessitate assuming an overdeveloped and institutional definition to the office of elder.

Still another approach is to read the directive to call the elders of the church as a way of circumventing charismatic healers. However, such a view is difficult to defend. While assuming the widespread nature of the gift of healing in early Christianity may be safe, concluding that the instruction to call for the elders of the church is a polemic against charismatic healers is a weight that the argument from silence may not be able to bear.

A final approach discusses the role of the elder without bringing in the matter of a healing gift at all. Unfortunately, this method does not do justice to the issue of healing in early Christianity, nor the reason for specifically requesting the elders to minister in such situations.

Thus, it appears safe to conclude that the elders were to be called because they were recognized leaders in the church. As such, they represent the community and its ability to minister to those who are physically ill. Healing ministry is not restricted to the elders, however, as verse 16 makes clear. Here the body of believers is encouraged to pray for one another in order that healings might occur. Whether or not James and his church were familiar with the gifts of the Spirit as defined in the Pauline literature, it is likely that at least one or more of the elders was recognized as having been used by God to facilitate the healing of individuals.

This assessment is based in part on the prominence of healing miracles in the New Testament accounts. The Gospels describe the empowerment of and mandates given to the disciples, and through them the readers of the Gospels, to heal the sick specifically (Matthew 10:1, 8; Mark 6:13; Luke 9:2, 6, 11; 10:9). The Book of Acts narrates extraordinary healings through a variety of individuals (3:7; 5:16; 8:7; 9:34; 14:8-10; 19:12; 28:8, 9). Several of the Epistles also assume that healings were part and parcel of the church's proclamation (e.g., 1 Corinthians 12:9; 1 Peter 2:24).

If, on the one hand, James was working with a conception of the gift of healing anything like that of Paul,[7] then in all likelihood one or more of the elders and perhaps one or more of the congregation at large were known for their healing gifts.[8] On the other hand, if James was writing before the Pauline idea of the gift of healing had emerged, or if James and his community pursued a distinctively non-Pauline approach in this regard, it is still likely that members of both the group of elders and the congregation would have been involved in healings such as those described in the Gospels and Acts.[9] The specific duties of the elders in these situations are to offer prayer, to anoint the sick person with oil, and to do it all in the name of the Lord.

Anoint with oil. Just before the prayer is offered, the elders are to anoint the sick person with oil. Despite questions surrounding the origin and meaning of this act, it should be noted that its mention by James gives the impression that he was not instituting something new but was describing an action with which his readers were familiar. What, then, is the purpose of anointing with oil?

In the Old Testament, anointing with oil is found in a variety of contexts. It was used in conjunction with the coronation of kings (1 Samuel 9:16), the consecra-

---

[7] That the Petrine community had such an exposure is at least suggested by 1 Peter 4:10, 11.

[8] One of the points on which James and Paul agree is that healings are to take place within the Christian community, the body of Christ.

[9] For evidence that healings continued in the early church long beyond the first century, cf. R.A.N. Kydd, *Charismatic Gifts in the Early Church* (Peabody, Mass.: Hendrickson, 1984), especially pp. 26, 44, 49, 54, 59, and 61. See also R. MacMullen, *Christianizing the Roman Empire A.D. 100-400* (New Haven, Conn.: Yale University Press, 1984).

tion of priests (Exodus 29:7), the calling of a prophet (1 Kings 19:16), the consecration of sacred objects (Exodus 30:22-29), and the treatment of wounds (Isaiah 1:6) and/or disease (Leviticus 14:15-18). In later rabbinic thought (*Mishnah*, Sabbath 23:5), anointing with oil could even be used as part of the preparation of the dead for burial.

The nearest parallel to the admonition given in James 5:14, however, is found in Mark 6:13, where it is recorded that the Twelve, having been sent out by Jesus, cast out many demons and anointed many sick people with oil. A clear distinction is drawn between exorcisms and healings, with oil being used in the latter. While oil had medicinal associations in antiquity, it appears that the anointing with oil described in Mark 6:13 served as a symbol of God's healing power. Bo Reicke goes so far as to say that the disciples had received a mandate from Jesus to anoint with oil.[10] The similarities between the practice in Mark 6:13 and James 5:14 indicate anointing with oil was based on a directive of Jesus, or on the action of His disciples.

It is possible to define the use of oil in medicinal terms, but the similarities of James 5:14 to Mark 6:13 and the context of healing as an answer to the prayers of the elders and people rule out this option. The possibility that mention of oil is an indication that James was describing an exorcism seems even further from the mark. James, who exhibited a knowledge of demons, could certainly have given his instructions in exorcism terminology if he had so chosen. Further, Mark 6:13 clearly differentiates between exorcisms

---

[10]Bo Reicke, "L'onction des malades d'apre's Saint Jacques," *La Maison-Dieu* 113 (1973), p. 51.

and healings. Least likely is the possibility that James mentioned anointing with oil in connection with extreme unction, since the purpose for the anointing he described is to bring healing and preserve life, not to prepare for death.

Inasmuch as the anointing is to function alongside prayer, and healing is not dependent on the anointing with oil (as verse 16 makes clear), it is likely that the anointing with oil serves as some kind of sign. Since the significance of the act is not specified in either Mark or James, it is probable that the use of oil as a sign incorporated some of the meaning it had come to have generally. Given its many associations with medicine, it seems natural that oil would serve as a sign of healing. In this case, however, the healing would not be the direct result of the oil but would be of supernatural origin.

But such general associations with healing do not exhaust the richness of this sign nor fully explain the rationale behind the choice of oil as the sign. By the first century, oil had come to have more powerful associations with healing. Several ancient sources express the idea that oil obtained from the tree in Paradise had healing virtues and implied that such oil would again become available in the messianic age.[11] Obviously, James did not regard the oil as having healing virtues in and of itself. However, the associations which oil had come to have with healing generally, and eschatological healing in particular, suggests that its presence in Jesus' ministry and in the practice of the early church signified the power of God to

---

[11] *Life of Adam and Eve* (93); *The Acts of Pilate* (19); *The Apocalypse of Moses* (9); 4 Ezra 2:12.

heal. This was one implication of the inauguration of the kingdom of God.

Consequently, oil was a powerful reminder to the church that God was able to heal and that His healing powers were already being made manifest. Such an eschatological emphasis fits the use of oil in the context of Mark 6:13 well, for the Twelve were sent to preach conversion (v. 12) because the kingdom of God was near.

In the name of the Lord. The anointing is to be done "in the name of the Lord." This qualification clearly designates the action as a religious anointing and distinguishes it from magical rites of the day. But how should "in the name of the Lord" be understood? Does the use of the name carry a potent efficacy on its own? Does its use verify that the individual who uses the name is a representative of the Lord? Or does the phrase "in the name of the Lord" specify the one who is to anoint, or the kind of oil to be used?

It should be remembered that the words of Jesus in John's Gospel include directives to make requests "in my name" (14:13, 14; 16:23). Such a tradition prompts Bietenhard to conclude:

> It is in obedience to Jesus (ἐν τῷ ὀνόματι τοῦ κυρίου) that the sick in the church are healed by anointing with oil (Jeremiah. 5:14f.), for Jesus has pledged his disciples to mutual assistance. Healing does not take place by pronouncing a set formula, but through the Lord in answer to the prayer which calls upon Him in faith.[12]

---

[12]H. Bietenhard, "ὄνομα," *TDNT* V, p. 278.

A variety of other things in early Christianity are also either done or commanded to be done in Jesus' name. These include baptism (Acts 2:38; 8:16; 10:48), exorcism (Matthew 7:22; Mark 9:38; Luke 10:17; Acts 16:18), healing (Acts 3:6; 4:10), speaking boldly (Acts 9:28), assembling (1 Corinthians 5:4), giving thanks (Ephesians 5:20), being justified (1 Corinthians 6:11), and giving commands (2 Thessalonians 3:6). In fact, Paul went so far as to say that whatever one does should be done in the name of the Lord Jesus (Colossians 3:17).

Reference to the Lord's name is also found in James 5:10, where suffering saints are exhorted to follow the example of the prophets who, despite such afflictions, "spoke in the name of the Lord." This use of the phrase seems to convey the idea of speaking with the authority of the Lord or in His behalf. The close proximity of these phrases in James, the implication of Mark 6:13 that Jesus himself had instructed the disciples to anoint with oil, the role of the elders as representatives of the community, and the significance of the anointing itself all suggest that to anoint "in the name of the Lord" meant to act in conformity to the Lord's directives and on His behalf as eschatological agents. It is possible that the words of Jesus in John's Gospel concerning prayer serve as a secondary reason for this action.

Verse 15

Following the anointing with oil, but in close conjunction with it, the elders are instructed to offer prayer. More specifically, they are to offer the prayer "in faith."

The prayer of faith will save the sick. Several aspects of this verse are worthy of comment: (1) Reference to the prayer of faith seems to indicate that it is the prayer and not the oil that results in healing. (2) Since it is the prayer offered by the elders which is demanded, it appears that their faith is being emphasized. (3) Only in this verse in the whole of the New Testament does the Greek word used here (εὐχῇ) mean "prayer."[13]

"The prayer of faith" may be defined in terms of the epistle itself. James made clear that when someone in need makes a request of the Lord, such a petition should be made with the confident expectation that God will hear and answer the prayer (1:5-8). To doubt that God will respond to the prayer is to be double-minded. A person who doubts will not receive any-thing from God. Therefore, to offer the prayer of faith is the opposite of doubting and/or being double-mind-ed. Such a bold statement might be taken to imply that prayer offered without doubt must certainly result in receiving that which is requested. James indicated else-where, however, that the prayer of faith must be accompanied by proper motives. Selfish prayers or those offered for other wrong motives mean the peti-tioner will not receive what is requested (4:3).

In this particular case, "the prayer of faith will save the sick and the Lord will raise him up." While in four occurrences in James (1:21; 2:14; 4:12; 5:20) the Greek word translated "save" (σώζω) has a soteriological or eschatological meaning, it is best to conclude that here in James 5:15 it refers to physical healing. This conclu-sion is based on its meaning in other New Testament

---

[13]In its other two occurrences it means a vow (Acts 18:18; 21:23), although *euche* is used for prayer in classical Greek. Cf. J.C. Thomas, "Euche," The Complete Bible Library: *The New Testament Greek-English Dictionary, Delta—Epsilon*, ed. T. Gilbrant (Springfield: Complete Biblical Library, 1990), pp. 658-59.

passages,[14] its use in the Greek papyri,[15] and its context.

While "to raise up" can also be used to refer to resurrection,[16] it is commonly used to describe the effects of a physical healing in the New Testament,[17] and most scholars take it in that sense here. Clearly, one aspect of the elders' prayer is for the physical healing of those who call for prayer.

If sin has been committed, it will be forgiven. In addition to healing for the body, the sick person will receive forgiveness of sin, if needed.

The background of this verse appears to be a belief in Judaism that there was often a direct connection between sin and sickness. The Old Testament evidence for this connection is plentiful. The idea is found in the Torah (Deuteronomy 28:20-27), the Psalms (Psalm 38), the Prophets (Isaiah 38:17), and the Wisdom Literature (numerous places in Job). It is also found in extrabiblical literature nearer to the time of the New Testament (*Sirach* 18:19-21; *Testament of the Twelve Patriarchs*—Reuben 1:7; Simeon 2:12; Zebulon 5:4; and Gad 5:9-10). Claims that the Jews always made such a connection are not well founded, however. H.H. Rowley concludes that while there may be innocent suffering in the Old Testament, not all suffering is innocent. "The Bible never tries to reduce the facts of experience to the simplicity the theorist seeks."[18]

---

[14]Cf. the meaning of σώζω in Matthew 9:21; Mark 5:28, 34; 6:56; 10:52; and Luke 8:48.

[15]Cf. A. Deissmann, *Light From the Ancient East*, p. 181, note 8.

[16]Cf. 1 Corinthians 15:15, 16, 29, 32, 35, 42-44, 52; 2 Corinthians 1:9; 4:14.

[17]Cf. Matthew 9:5-7, 25; Mark 1:31; 2:9, 11-12; 5:41; 9:27; Acts 3:6, 7.

[18]H.H. Rowley, *The Faith of Israel* (London: SCM Press, 1956), p.114. Cf. also his comments on pp. 115-116.

James makes it clear that while sin may be the reason for sickness, sin is not always the reason for it. One cannot merely assume that sickness is the direct result of sin. Apparently, the sick person is the one who knows whether an illness is the result of sin, as James advocates confession of sins to one another in order to receive healing. Neither a private confession to the elders nor an expectation that the elders should discern the sin is implied. It appears that the sin would not be something about which the sick person would have any doubts, but rather would be apparent. There is no hint that those whose illness is not the direct result of sin are presumed guilty of sin until proven innocent, nor are they under pressure to conjure up some fault.

This question remains, however, in those cases where sin is the direct cause of sickness: What is the precise nature of the causal relationship? Although a number of passages in the New Testament attribute some illnesses to the effects of demon possession, there is no evidence that this is what James had in mind. His knowledge of demons (2:19) and the devil's activity (4:7) suggest that he possibly knew of individuals who as a result of the devil were bound by disease. But James does not give the slightest hint about such a possibility here. If James attributed such sickness to demons, it is odd that he was not explicit about this matter in the one place in the whole New Testament where the clearest directives concerning healing and the resulting forgiveness are found.

Rather, James' words are best understood against the backdrop of the Old Testament and its affirmations about the relationship between sin and sickness.

The Old Testament clearly regards God himself as the author of the punishment for sin generally. In those passages where there is an explicit connection made between sin and sickness, God is also invariably the One responsible for the illness (see Leviticus 26:14-16; Numbers 12:9, 10; 2 Kings 5:27; 2 Chronicles 21:12-15; Psalm 38). Given the Jewish orientation of the Epistle of James and the extent to which sickness resulting from sin was attributed to God in the first century, the most plausible explanation regarding the relationship between sin and sickness in James 5:15 is that God is responsible for certain illnesses.

That some sickness is the result of sin might be implied because the Greek word (πεποιηκώ) used here is in the perfect tense: "If he has committed sin [in the past with the effects still felt], it will be forgiven him."

Verse 16

Confess your sins. In the light of the fact that sometimes illness is the direct result of sin, and the prayer of faith is instrumental in both healing and forgiveness. "Therefore confess your sins to one another and pray for one another." Confession of sin is well known in the Old Testament for the individual (Leviticus 5:5; Numbers 5:7; Job 33:26-28; Psalms 32:5; 38:3, 4; 40:12; 51:3-5; Proverbs 20:9; 28:13) and for the community (Leviticus 16:21; 26:40; Daniel 9:4-11). According to Gerhard von Rad, two elements are involved in confession: (1) the confession (or acknowledgment) of sin and (2) the praise of God.

> In accepting a justly imposed judgment, the man confesses transgression, and he clothes what he

says in the mantle of an avowal giving God the glory. The essence of this and of every act of praise is that in all circumstances it declares God to be in the right.[19]

Confession of sin was remarkably widespread in early Christianity as well (Matthew 3:6; Mark 1:5; Acts 19:18; 1 John 1:9; see also other early church writings: 1 Clement 51:3; 52:1; Didache 4:14; 14:1; Barnabas 19:12; Hermas, Visions 1, 1:3; 3, 1:5, 6; Similitude 9, 23:4). The confession of sin advocated by James is not simply a general confession, but rather a confession of those sins which were thought to have resulted in illness. At the very least, such confession would function as "preventive medicine." While it is possible to interpret the confession as a private act either to elders or to fellow believers who had been wronged by a brother or sister, in all likelihood James was calling for a public confession of particular sins not unlike that implied in other early Christian documents.[20] The mutual and fraternal confession of sin is for the specific purpose of intercession. James implied that individual believers are spiritually accountable for one another. This idea is similar to John's admonition to his readers in 1 John 5:16, 17.

Pray for one another. On hearing the specific sins and needs of a brother or sister, the believer is to petition God on behalf of the confessor. Such prayers should result in healing. Some commentators argue

---

[19]Gerhard von Rad, *Old Testament Theology* I (trans. D.M.G. Stalker; New York: Harper and Row, 1962), p. 359.

[20]On the nature of public confession in early Christianity, cf. the discussion in R.E. Brown, *The Epistles of John* (Garden City: Doubleday, 1982), p. 208, and J.C. Thomas, *Footwashing in John 13 and the Johannine Community* (JSNTS 61; Sheffield, England: JSOT Press, 1991), p. 185.

that a "spiritual" healing is described in verse 16, noting that the Greek word (ἰάομαι) is sometimes used metaphorically for healing in the New Testament. But this interpretation does not do justice to the evidence for several reasons:

1. Verse 16 is closely connected to the preceding discussion about physical healing by the use of "therefore."

2. The same Greek word appears frequently in the Greek papyri in contexts which describe physical healing.

3. This word takes on a spiritual application in the New Testament only when it appears in quotations from the Old Testament. Therefore, it is better to take the term (ἰάομαι) as having reference to physical healing.

The prayer of a righteous person accomplishes much. James ends this verse with the exhortation that the prayer of a righteous person accomplishes much. Instead of taking "righteous" as referring to individuals of extraordinary faith, James was emphasizing the ordinariness of those who offer prayer. This is clear from the qualifying statement that "Elijah was a man of like passions" (v. 17). Instead of importing a definition of *righteous* into James 5:16, the most reasonable course of action is to allow James' use of the term in other contexts to guide its meaning here. In his epistle, *righteous* and its cognates designate belief. In the case of Abraham or Rahab, it is not simply faith, but faith manifested by its works (cf. James 2:21 with 1:20; 2:24 with 2:23; 2:25 with 3:18). The righteous person described here is one who does those things which are pleasing to God and in conformity to His will. This is no small order, to be sure; but

James implied it is within the reach of every believer. The description of Joseph in Matthew 1:19 is perhaps as good an example of this understanding of "righteous" as one finds in the New Testament.

The author commends the power of prayer by the combination of "much" "strength" and "that which works." It is difficult to avoid the conclusion that James regarded prayer as a powerful resource for the believer and the church when faced with illnesses. The admonition about prayer and faith in James 1:6-8 dovetails with this strong affirmation concerning the power of prayer.

James closed this passage by pointing to Elijah's success in prayer as an example to encourage his readers.

Summary and Conclusions

This brief analysis of James 5:14-16 cannot begin to answer all the questions surrounding the devil, disease, and deliverance in New Testament thought. Several conclusions emerge, however.

1. *James 5:14-16 clearly regards some illnesses as being the direct result of sin.* While James offered some qualification of this statement, the fact that sin and sickness are connected so explicitly should not be ignored nor softened.

2. *When sickness is the direct result of sin, confession of that sin is required.* Such confession is to be made at least to fellow believers for the specific purpose of intercession. There is no indication that the sick believer is to be preoccupied with discovering some secret sin that may have been committed; rather, the implication is that the sick believer would know full well the nature of the sin. The impression is left that confession should be a normal part of the

worshiping community's life. The fact that there is no place for such confession in many contemporary churches is more an indication of the church's superficiality and fragmentation than it is a sign of the early church's naiveté or lack of sophistication.

3. *James advocated a continuing ministry of healing, which incorporates the anointing with oil by the elders and praying fervently that healing will result.* James did not consider the possibility that healing might not be attained.

4. *It is also remarkably clear that James did not consider all illness to be the direct result of sin.* This may imply that certain illnesses are simply the consequence of living in a sinful world. In such cases the sick believers are not presumed to be guilty of sin until proven innocent.

5. *In keeping with much Old Testament thought, James seems to imply that sicknesses which accompany sin are the direct result of God's own activity.*

How do the positions represented by the three categories with which this chapter opened fare when compared to these initial conclusions? Those in the first category seem vindicated in their no nonsense approach of offering fervent prayer for the sick and in their discerning that some illnesses are the direct result of sin. However, they appear to have erred in assuming that all illness is to be attributed to sin and /or the devil. If some illnesses are the direct result of divine intervention, the absolute attribution of all illness to sin or the devil might draw very near to blasphemy of the Spirit, which according to Mark is attributing the works of God to the devil. At the very least, it cautions against the cursing of every illness as a satanic intrusion, if it is possible that the source is God and not the devil. More discernment is also needed in praying for the sick, in that it is possible for Christians to ask amiss in prayer.

Members of the second group have accurately discerned that not every illness may be directly attributed to the devil and that it is possible to ask with the wrong motives. However, many in this category have not taken seriously enough the fact that some sickness may be the direct result of sin and may come as chastisement from God. Many in this group probably offer prayers in a less-than-fervent manner. Perhaps some have not received healing due to a lack of appreciation for one of these two dimensions.

The so-called "functional deists" have erred more than the other two groups combined. On the one hand, they have not because they ask not. Since they rarely pray fervently, they fall into the trap of being "double-minded" (1:8). On the other hand, illnesses which should call their attention to the presence of sin in their lives may many times go unnoticed, as such sicknesses are routinely attributed to "natural causes."

Suggestions for Further Study

Many other sections of the New Testament contain information crucial to a comprehensive understanding of this topic. Six additional areas of exploration appear to be most promising for research and study.

1. *Pauline Literature.* Of particular relevance for this topic is Paul's teaching regarding the gifts of healings; his statement in 1 Corinthians 11:30-32 that many of the Corinthians were sick and some had

even died because they were abusing the Lord's Table; and the attitude he expressed toward illness, whether his own or that of those with whom he worked.

2. *Johannine Literature.* Three passages in the Johannine literature are of special significance for this theme:

John 5:14: Jesus admonished the man healed at the Pool of Bethesda to stop sinning lest something worse than his previous infirmity fall on him.[21]

John 9:3: In response to the disciples' question regarding the cause of the blind man's condition, Jesus stated that the blindness occurred so that the works of God might be done in him.

3 John 2: The Elder expressed his desire for the health and prosperity of Gaius.

3. *Mark.* In addition to Mark's treatment of the relationship between demon possession and illness, the passage in 2:1-12 depicts Jesus pronouncing forgiveness of sin immediately before healing a paralytic. This story deserves special attention.

4. *Matthew.* The relationship between demon possession and illness and the way in which Scripture is fulfilled through suffering appear to be strategic.

5. *Luke-Acts.* A careful examination of Jesus' attitude and that of the disciples toward sickness, the relationship of illness to demon possession, and God's own role in inflicting suffering and death on those who sin are also possible themes to examine.

---

[21]See J.C. Thomas, "'Stop Sinning Lest Something Worse Come Upon You': The Man at the Pool in John 5," *Journal for the Study of the New Testament* 59 (1995), pp. 3-20.

6. *Revelation.* Although generally regarded as part of the Johannine literature, Revelation deserves separate attention because of its distinctive testimony about the role of suffering and the part that God and Satan play in afflicting and punishing both saints and sinners.

While other portions of the New Testament might also shed light upon this topic, and while additional areas within the documents cited here might be of special significance, perhaps enough of an outline has been given to suggest the shape and extent of the work that lies before us.[22]

---

[22]For a more detailed version of this study, see J.C. Thomas, "The Devil, Disease, and Deliverance: James 5:14-16," *Journal of Pentecostal Theology* 2 (1993), pp. 25-50.

LEADERSHIP AND INTEGRITY: LESSONS FROM THE JOHANNINE EPISTLES

Not long ago a colleague told me of a situation in which a minister had obtained a job under false pretenses. My response betrayed my own disillusionment with such tactics. Doesn't anyone tell the truth anymore? Unfortunately, practices such as this are all too common these days. Whether it involves greed, sexual immorality, or the desire for power, the crisis exists at every level of the church—local parishes, denominational leadership, missionary organizations, televangelists, parachurch ministries, and seminaries and Bible colleges.

While we are all better at removing the speck from our brother or sister's eye than removing the beam from our own, I cannot help but believe we need to be encouraged to evaluate our own lives and reflect critically on the presence or absence of integrity in them.

One of the best ways to gauge one's integrity is to observe a person under the extreme pressure of a crisis. In times of adversity one's true nature is revealed—as basic instincts, such as self-preservation, take over. The way one handles problems, challenges, and attacks reveals much about one's sense of personal integrity, as well as one's integrity as a leader.

There are of course, a number of places in the Bible to which one might turn for case studies of how various leaders faced adversity. Rather than reexamining the well-known apostle Paul—who maintained great integrity in spite of many severe trials—I have chosen to lift up a leader in the early church who has received much less attention: John the Elder, who wrote the Johannine Epistles.

The Johannine literature is a distinctive part of the New Testament Canon. These documents—the Gospel of John; 1, 2, 3 John; and Revelation—not only show signs of connection but also give evidence that they were written at different times. This chapter will give an overview of the Johannine literature and survey the history and character of the community that produced it. Following this orientation will be an exegetical and theological reading of 3 John 9, 10 and an analysis of the Elder's response to the crisis in the community. A final section seeks to collate any conclusions and identify the implications of this study for the present situation.

The Johannine Literature

A comparison of the Johannine Epistles with the Gospel of John reveals a number of similarities. The similarities are so great in terms of vocabulary, style, and theology that these documents appear to come from the same community, if not from the same author. For this reason, it is advantageous to interpret the epistles in the light of their relationship to the Fourth Gospel.

What is the exact nature of this relationship, and what are its implications? There is reason to believe that the Gospel of John existed, in some form, prior to the composition of the epistles.[1] The primary evidence is the fact that the epistles, especially 1 John, seem to presuppose the existence of the Fourth Gospel. While no passage from the Gospel is directly quoted in his epistles, several passages in the latter appear to build on those in the former.[2]

Another piece of evidence which supports this chronological order is that 1 John reflects a different kind of life situation than that of the Fourth Gospel. The epistles appear to have been written when the community was torn by strife, a situation not suggested by the Fourth Gospel.

An additional reason to believe the epistles presuppose the Gospel is that even the opponents addressed in 1 John seem to base their beliefs on the

---

[1] It appears that the Fourth Gospel took shape over a long period of time. It is possible that the bulk of the Gospel was complete but had not been published in its final form when the epistles were written.

[2] Cf., for example, the way in which the prologue in 1 John 1:1-4 seems to build off its counterpart in John 1:1-18.

Fourth Gospel. Therefore, there is some wisdom in reading the epistles with one eye on the Gospel.

The Johannine Community

If the Gospel and the epistles come from the same hand and/or community, and if the churches addressed in these epistles are under the oversight and influence of the Elder (a title the author of 2 and 3 John used for himself), then it is legitimate to speak of a community of disciples and churches. They are known as the Johannine community.

It is clear from the Gospel that standing at the heart of the community's life was the Beloved Disciple. According to the Fourth Gospel, the Beloved Disciple was an eyewitness to the earthly ministry of Jesus, and his testimony formed the basis of the community's belief in Jesus, (especially note John 19:35 and 21:24.) From the evidence in the Gospel, it may be deduced that the Beloved Disciple was a prominent teacher and that his role as an eyewitness attracted several disciples around him.

In one sense, then, to speak of the Johannine community is simply to identify the Beloved Disciple and his followers as constituting a clearly defined group. The epistles demonstrate, however, that this community was larger than the one group gathered around the Beloved Disciple. It appears that several churches were part of this community and that they all came under his influence in one way or another.

History of the Johannine Community

Based on evidence contained in the Johannine literature and information found in Christian writers of the second century, a provisional outline of the history of the Johannine community may be delineated. It can be divided into four phases or periods.[3]

The earliest period in the history of the community is the point at which the Beloved Disciple, an eyewitness to Jesus' ministry, left Jerusalem or Palestine and took up residence in or around Ephesus in Asia Minor. This migration probably occurred sometime in the mid to late 60s of the first century A.D. The Beloved Disciple's departure was in all likelihood related to the turmoil prior to or at the beginning of the first Jewish war, in A.D. 66-70 against Rome. The Beloved Disciple was no doubt accompanied by other believers.

The second phase in the community's history was the establishment of the community proper and its initial growth. During this period, the Fourth Gospel began to take shape through the preaching and teaching of the Beloved Disciple. His testimony was especially cherished, as he was one of the few remaining eyewitnesses of Jesus' ministry. From circa A.D. 70 to 90 the Fourth Gospel continued to develop.

Phase three in the community's history saw the disruption of the community, possibly because of the absence of the Beloved Disciple who may have been imprisoned on Patmos. The community appears to have split into at least two parts. The Elder (who in all likelihood is to be identified as the Beloved Disciple) wrote the epistles in an attempt to solidify those still loyal to the truth, and to defend the Gospel as it was rightly to be understood. In all likelihood these works were written circa A.D. 100.

The final phase in the community's history wit-

---

[3]For a similar but more exhaustive treatment of this topic, see Martin Hengel, *The Johannine Question* (Philadelphia: Trinity International Press, 1989).

nessed the death of the Beloved Disciple, the publication of the Fourth Gospel in its final form, and the absorption of the community into the emerging church. The opponents discussed in the epistles followed the path leading to Gnosticism.

Consequently, the Johannine Epistles were written at a crucial point in the history of the community, and their proper interpretation depends in part on an appreciation of their context. As we continue our study, it is imperative to read the epistles with a constant focus on the community's history.

3 John

Third John is the shortest book in the New Testament. It consists of only 219 words in the Greek text. Its brevity, more than any other factor, is the reason for its location behind 1 and 2 John in the Canon. New Testament documents by the same authors were commonly arranged by length, in descending order.[4] As such, 3 John would have easily fit on a single sheet of papyrus, the normal length of Greco-Roman letters of the day, the equivalent of the modern-day postcard.[5] Not only does 3 John resemble a number of secular Greco-Roman letters in its brevity, but it also shares a number of structural and literary features.[6] Such similarities demonstrate that we are dealing with an authentically private piece of correspondence.

---

[4]Although 3 John is divided into 15 verses, as compared to 2 John's 13, 3 John is some 26 words shorter.

[5]Hengel, p. 29.

[6]Among the similarities which 3 John shares with Greco-Roman letters of the first century are the A to B greeting (v. 1), the wish for health (v. 2), the expression of joy or thanksgiving (vv. 3, 4), the occasion (vv. 5-8), the petition (vv. 9-12), the closing (vv. 13, 14), and a concluding formula (v. 14).

Third John offers a most intriguing glimpse into the Johannine community. The letter reveals a group of congregations tied together by a series of messengers/emissaries. It also reveals a rift in the community particularly between the Elder and Diotrephes.[7]

To understand the purpose of 3 John, the roles of the only three members of the Johannine community whose names we know must be explored. The following minimal information may be assumed about each.

Simply put, *Gaius* was the one to whom the letter was written; *Diotrephes* was an antagonist/opponent of the Elder; and *Demetrius* was being commended by the Elder to Gaius. But a closer examination reveals a host of questions: What was the relationship of Gaius to the Elder? Who was Gaius and what was his position? What was the relationship of Diotrephes to the Elder? Why did he oppose the Elder? What was his position or authority? What was Demetrius' function? If Gaius had offered hospitality to emissaries of the Elder, why was the Elder so worried about Demetrius' reception? Why was he concerned that Gaius would withdraw such support?

While a certain amount of ambiguity may exist concerning the answer to some of these questions, the purpose of 3 John is certain: The Elder wrote concerning the need for Gaius to continue in the ministry of hospitality within the community. This purpose is

---

[7] If one relies on 1 and 2 John to determine the cause of the rift, the conclusion would involve false teaching, which is so prominently discussed in these other Johannine Epistles. One searches 3 John in vain, however, for the slightest hint of heresy. No one would even suspect that false teaching was at issue if 3 John existed on its own. Such arguments from silence are all the more difficult in the light of the Elder's willingness to condemn false teaching and his eagerness to combat it at every point.

made clear in verses 5-8, 11, and 12.

While it is beyond the scope of this study to consider every point of the various hypotheses offered as answers to these questions, it should be noted that at least seven different proposals have been made concerning the identity of Diotrephes alone!

1. One view is that Diotrephes was the first person known to have striven to be a monarchical bishop, anticipating the stance of Ignatius by a few years. The Elder, who came from a less structured, more charismatic background, disdained such love of prominence.

2. Another approach simply inverts the roles of Diotrephes and the Elder.

3. Another view identifies Diotrephes as a wealthy member of the Johannine community who hosted a Johannine congregation (house church) in his home. Wealthier members of early Christian communities often hosted the house church for the simple reason that their homes could ordinarily accommodate more people.

4. It is common to assume that Diotrephes was one of the heretics/false teachers so severely condemned in 1 and 2 John. The obvious problem here is that 3 John gives no hint that this is the case.

5. One scholar has gone so far as to argue that Diotrephes was an orthodox church leader while the Elder was an excommunicated heretic.

6. Another hypothesis asserts that the Elder and Diotrephes were on the same side against false teaching but disagreed over the best way to handle the false teachers. The Elder advocated discernment, while Diotrephes refused to admit any traveling teachers.

7. Finally, one scholar has proposed that the tension between the Elder and Diotrephes was simply the result of a misunderstanding.

a. An anonymous teacher claimed a revelation in the Spirit that deviated from the Elder, and this teacher began to travel in the name of the Elder.

b. Diotrephes discerned the heretical content of the teaching and decided if that was the Elder's position, he (*Diotrephes*) would have nothing else to do with the Elder or his emissaries.

c. The Elder penned 3 John as a rebuke, not knowing the full story.

d. The letter was followed up by a visit, which was threatened in verse 10.

e. The Elder and Diotrephes discovered what had happened.

f. The Elder agreed with Diotrephes' strategy in combatting false teachers (see 2 John 10, 11).

Hospitality in the Early Church

The New Testament documents suggest that there was a high degree of mobility in early Christianity. Travel was not easy, however, in terms of the physical energies required or in accommodations along the way. Most inns of the time were quite unreliable and notorious for vices that were repugnant to Christians. Consequently, believers were often hard-pressed to find suitable accommodations. People who knew folks along the way would ordinarily attempt to establish their own network of places to stay.[8] Therefore, hospitality generally became part of standard Christian practice in many segments of the early church.

This was necessary not only because it was an expression of Christian faith but also because successful

---

[8]J. Lieu, *The Second and Third Epistles of John* (Edinburgh: T. & T. Clark, 1986), p. 126.

evangelization efforts by itinerant prophets and ministers were dependent on such support (Matthew 10:11-15; Acts 16:15; Romans 16:1, 2; 3 John 5-8).[9] Without the generous hospitality of individual believers like Gaius, those in the church who were devoting their efforts to evangelism would be hard-pressed to continue. Specifically, the Elder's call for hospitality would involve provisions during the evangelists' stay and appropriate supplies for their journey, such as food, money, and in some cases even the washing of their clothes. Such a constant undertaking on Gaius' part would be no small affair and would require both means and will.

A careful examination of 3 John 9, 10 reveals the reason the Elder made this request of Gaius and shows much about the nature of the conflict between Diotrephes and the Elder.

An Examination of 3 John 9, 10

Although the Elder had already made his petition known to Gaius, he now revealed the occasion of the letter itself. That occasion concerned the actions of Diotrephes, his authority in the church, and his relationship with the Elder. Verse 9 reveals that apparently the Elder had earlier written a short letter (the significance of τι)[10] to the church.[11] Although that letter no longer exists, it is likely that it was a commendation of a missionary/traveler. However, the one who loved to be first among them (Diotrephes) refused the Elder by refusing his letter.

---

[9]See J.C. Thomas, *Footwashing in John 13 and the Johannine Community*, p. 135.
[10]Attempts to identify this composition with either 1 or 2 John both fail.
[11]Obviously, "the church" mentioned here and in verse 10 is not the same congregation mentioned earlier in verse 6.

The word translated "the one who loves to be first" (ὁ φιλοπρωτεύων) is unique in the New Testament. While use of the word charges that Diotrephes loved prominence in the community, further details about the meaning are difficult to come by. It could be that Diotrephes had become, or aspired to become, a bishop. The Elder, who opposed either institutionalization or the elevation of Diotrephes, was against such a move. Another view identifies Diotrephes with false teaching so that his rejection of the Elder was the result of theological differences. Perhaps it is more reasonable to view Diotrephes as a zealous member of the community whose leadership skills had resulted in a position of authority in the church. He certainly appears to have a variety of powers, according to verse 10.

Unfortunately, Diotrephes had a moral flaw: he loved to be first. Such an attitude was difficult to understand in a community accustomed to the example of John the Baptist, among others, who exemplified humility in terms of self-estimation. The fact that the phrase "the one who loves to be first" (ὁ φιλοπρωτεύων αὐτῶν) precedes Diotrephes' name in the Greek text heightens the force of this accusation. This moral flaw manifested itself in a constant refusal to receive the Elder's authority.[12] While not guilty of the sort of false teaching described in 1 and 2 John, Diotrephes' ambition resulted in a violation of the ethical and theological commitments of the community. His actions demonstrate that he had broken fel-

---

[12]It is possible that the word *them* (αὐτῶν) should be taken to imply that Gaius was not a part of Diotrephes' congregation, as *them* (αὐτῶν) rather than *us* (ἡμῶν) appears.

lowship with the larger community; he did not obey the command of love, a command central in the community's thinking.

Because Diotrephes would not receive the Johannine emissaries, the Elder announced in verse 10 that he planned a trip to make clear to the church what Diotrephes did and said, a course of action similar to that proposed by Paul in 2 Corinthians 12:14 and 13:1. Such a visit would allow the Elder to communicate to them everything that had transpired. This verse suggests that John had the authority to take such action.

Although some want to view Diotrephes as a pastor concerned about his congregation and those who visited it, verse 10 makes clear that the love of prominence was not Diotrephes' only fault. He habitually made accusations against the Elder, attempting to slander him and, perhaps, ruin his reputation. Not only did Diotrephes refuse to receive the Elder and continually slander him, but he also refused to receive the brothers. That Diotrephes was not content with actions directed toward the Elder alone, suggests that his treatment of others was determined in part by the way they related to John.

Diotrephes habitually refused to receive the Johannine missionaries. This refusal not only implies a rejection of the Elder's authority but would also effectively put an end to missionary work in that community.

What's more, Diotrephes felt such strong opposition to the Elder that he habitually forbade everyone in the community to receive his emissaries. The connection between the Elder and those who desired to receive the missionaries may be partial motivation for Diotrephes' action. But Diotrephes did not stop with these hostile actions. He went so far as to throw any sympathizers out of the church. While formal excommunication is not likely meant, the exclusion of these believers is somewhat similar to the action advocated by Jesus (Matthew 18:15-17) and by Paul's example (1 Corinthians 5:1-8). These two verses (3 John 8, 9) reveal that Diotrephes was guilty of four things:

1. He would not receive the Elder's letter.
2. He slandered the Elder and others with evil words.
3. He did not receive the brothers.
4. He threw out of the church anyone who aided the brothers.

The thrust of verses 9 and 10 makes clear the purpose for the letter: Gaius' hospitality is all the more important because of Diotrephes' actions. The letter suggests that Gaius' walking in the truth—that is, his ministry of hospitality—might be severely tested. It also makes clear that to stand with the Elder entails opposing Diotrephes. It is obvious that Diotrephes would meet anyone's attempt to withstand him with dangerous hostility.

The Elders Response to This Crisis

How did the Elder respond to what might appropriately be called open rebellion on the part of Diotrephes?

First, John attempted to keep the lines of communication open. This was done despite Diotrephes' actions against and attacks on the Elder. His efforts to maintain contact are documented by the fact that he had sent emissaries to the church where Diotrephes had influence. Following their rejection, the Elder had sent the church a letter, which was also repelled by Diotrephes. Apparently, other messengers were sent to the church who found an initial reception with individual members of the congregation, but Diotrephes again intervened by rejecting them (v. 10).

The sending of the letter itself (3 John) is still another part of the Elder's effort to keep in contact with the situation. The epistle even indicates the Elder's future plans to communicate with Diotrephes—a visit to sort things out in person.

Second, although the Elder possessed a good deal of personal authority as the founder and leader of the community[13] and had been an eyewitness to Jesus' ministry, he chose to ground his admonitions and response within the community context. The Elder subtly reminded Gaius of his own connection to the community by referring to his testimony among the brothers (vv. 3, 6). He emphasized Gaius' obligation to receive the Johannine missionaries as one believer among many (v. 8). The Elder also used the first person plural in order to identify with Gaius and to lift up the fact that the Elder himself was part of the larger Christian community (vv. 9, 12). Finally, the Elder emphasized the community context in the closing greetings conveyed from one congregation to another in verse 14 ("The friends greet you" [*NASB*]).

A third significant aspect of the Elder's response to

---

[13]Notice, for example, that he referred to himself as "the elder," rather than one of the elders, as might be expected from other uses of *elder* in reference to the Jerusalem church (Acts 11:30; 15:2, 4, 6, 22, 23; 16:4; 21:18), the Pauline mission (Acts 14:23; 20:14-38), the Pauline circle (1 Timothy 4:14; 5:17-19; Titus 1:5), and the Petrine churches (1 Peter 5:1).

this crisis is the way in which he confronted Diotrephes. His words were carefully chosen and his allegations were quite specific. Rather than returning Diotrephes' slander in kind, the Elder attempted to avoid ambiguity by identifying the ways in which Diotrephes had offended and strayed from both the Elder and the community. That such accusations were not mere verbiage spoken in the heat of the moment is evidenced by the Elder's intent to visit the church and speak with Diotrephes and the church in person.

A fourth aspect of the Elder's response to this crisis was to challenge Gaius to proper action. Gaius was to take care that he did not conform to the dangerous influence of Diotrephes. In the face of such a crisis, it is extremely important that the good example be imitated, rather than the evil one. The Elder's admonition to Gaius underscores the need for godly role models who are examples of integrity, even when the cost is great and the temptation to conform to a model lacking integrity might be enormous.

Throughout the epistle the Elder has appealed to and made frequent mention of "the truth" (vv. 1, 3, 4, 8, 12). This final aspect of the Elder's response is so subtle that it can be missed unless one remembers the broader context of the Johannine community. Specifically, Gaius is said "to walk in the truth" (v. 3). To walk is a familiar metaphor in the Johannine Epistles, occurring in 1 John 1:6, 7; 2:11; and 2 John 4, 6. Three ideas are present in its use:

1. Walking is tied to fellowship both positively (1 John 1:7) and negatively (1:6). "To walk" is paramount to having fellowship with.

2. To walk in truth is to live according to the commands of God/Jesus (2 John 6).

3. Since the greatest command in the Johannine community was to love one another (1 John 3:11), one's love toward the brothers was a sign that one was walking in the truth, whereas it is impossible to walk in the truth if one hates a brother (1 John 2:11).

Therefore, for the Elder to state that Gaius walked in the truth is to acknowledge that he had fellowship with Jesus. This fellowship is evidenced by the fact that he loved the brothers, most recently typified by his generous hospitality toward the brothers. The Elder's use of "the truth" demonstrates that for John there was a standard of conduct and faith[14] by which a believer may gauge his or her life. By his own action, the Elder showed that he himself walked in the truth, even in a crisis.

Conclusions and Implications

In 3 John we see two distinct models of leadership. Both teach their own lessons about integrity. The actions of these two leaders, John and Diotrephes, seem to diverge at nearly every point. Diotrephes loved to be first, and this attitude led to a variety of hostile actions. The Elder chose to speak as one of the community, despite the fact that he, above all in the community, could have appealed to his own authority as founder, leader, and eyewitness.

Diotrephes sought to cut himself off from those with whom he differed; the Elder sought to keep the lines of communication open. Diotrephes worked to keep others silent and in line with his own thought;

---

[14]It should be observed that for John there was no division between proper belief and proper action (theology and ethics).

the Elder sought to enlist others in the process of reconciliation and encouraged them to act in accordance with the truth. Diotrephes used threats and manipulation to secure his own desired goals; the Elder appealed to the responsibilities of the believers and spoke from the love command.

No doubt, most of us have worked with and/or for leaders who have exhibited some or all of the characteristics of Diotrephes. If so, these questions should prove helpful in our own reflection:

In these situations, have I followed the evil example, convincing myself that one must be prepared to act thus in order to "get ahead"?

When confronted with challenges to my authority, have I sought to malign my challenger and destroy his or her influence through slander or so-called sharing?

Am I prone to make attempts to control such situations by demanding absolute conformity to my strategy of dealing with the situation?

Do I attempt to alienate and isolate those with whom I disagree, thereby demeaning them and treating their personhood with contempt through my actions and attitudes?

Have I been tempted to mistreat or punish others because they are closely associated with a "political opponent"?

Finally, do I love to be "first among them"? How differently would I act and relate to others if I did not have this desire for such prominence? In what ways do I love to be first and why?

When questions like these are raised, it is much easier to remove the speck from our brothers' and sisters' eyes than it is to remove the beam from our own. But before looking around to locate the "guilty parties," perhaps we should look into the mirror of Scripture and reflect about the sin in our own hearts and the steps needed to conform to the truth.

If any of us struggle with such attitudes and actions, the example of the Elder offers a model of integrity for us to emulate. Fortunately, some of us have had the privilege of working for and with those who were like the Elder. In the light of John's example, we can legitimately raise these questions:

When confronted with a challenger who opposes my authority and viciously maligns me, how should I respond?

How can I ensure that I treat the friends of my challengers with love and respect?

What lessons does the example of the Elder teach, and what antidote did he provide for the love of prominence?

Finally, how strong is my commitment to "walk in the truth," even if I must suffer for my walk?

Perhaps ending this chapter as we began it is not a bad idea: Doesn't anyone tell the truth anymore?

It's an important question to ponder.

Sin and Holiness in 1 John

The presence of sin in the body of Christ is a serious matter! What is perhaps even more disturbing is the presence of sin among the church's leaders. I must confess that such a state of affairs is painful, confusing, and even frightening. What accounts for the recent string of spiritual tragedies in Pentecostalism, including our own denomination? Are these too-frequent occurrences an unfortunate, unrelated series of events no different from adversities the church has faced in the past? Can they be attributed to satanic attacks on key leaders in the church? Or are they the firstfruits of God's impending judgment of the Church of God for unconfessed sins, both personal and structural?

It is not easy to know how to respond to such questions, for they are threatening and explosive. But the way the church answers these questions and interprets these events may well determine the spiritual and moral future of the Church of God.

Aside from trying to ignore the moral crises in leadership, perhaps the easiest way out is simply to attribute these tragic events to the devil in a trite way. But such responses leave most of us cold, suggesting an unwillingness to reflect on this situation in a serious manner. They do little to answer the real question about how these things could happen. This line of reasoning is similar to the advice Screwtape gives to his nephew demon, Wormwood, in letter 3 of the Screwtape Letters, regarding the best way to keep his human subject from seeing himself as he should:

> Aggravate that most useful characteristic, the horror and neglect of the obvious. You must bring him to a condition in which he can practice self-examination for an hour without discovering any of those facts about himself which are perfectly clear to anyone who has ever lived in the same house with him or worked in the same office.[1]

While the devil no doubt deserves credit for moral leadership failures, I believe most of us are haunted by the suspicion that we all share in the guilt of these tragedies. While it is tempting to exonerate ourselves from such heinous culpability, closer scrutiny reveals our complicity with a system that, despite its best intentions, may actually contribute to the spiritual failure of its leaders. Lest this observation be taken as

---

[1]C.S. Lewis, *The Screwtape Letters* (Charlotte, N.C.: Commission Press, 1976), p. 29.

the generalizations of a young malcontent, let me identify some specific ways in which the system fails in this regard:

First, there is generally a lack of true accountability of leaders. Often the demands we place on our leaders cut them loose from local accountability, and most of the supervision given has to do with administrative nuts and bolts.

Second, we have not managed to remedy the sense of isolation inherent in many leadership positions. Fear of betrayal and a sense of aloneness adversely affect our spiritual well-being.

Third, the institutionally acceptable sins of arrogance, pride, political ambition, and greed have gone unchecked for so long that they are viewed as a given in the church's life.

Fourth, the implicit blessing given to "success," as if that were to be equated with God's will, has produced a pragmatism in which the end justifies the means.

Fifth, our preoccupation with public relations and image has resulted, at times, in our being more concerned with perception than reality.

Such candid language should not be interpreted as a blanket indictment against the church and its leadership. Rather, it is the honest musings of one of the sons of the church in the face of our present dilemma. It should be stated clearly that not all are susceptible to each of the temptations that result from our systemic weaknesses, but all of us are aware of those areas where, individually, we are most vulnerable to sin.

One way to respond positively to this desperate situation is to compare our own attitudes to sin with that of an early Christian community. The Johannine community was a group of churches in Asia Minor that was gathered around and under the oversight of the Beloved Disciple. These congregations included those implied in 1, 2, 3 John. They also included the seven listed in Revelation 2 and 3: Ephesus, Smyrna, Pergamum, Thyatira, Sardis, Philadelphia, and Laodicea. We will look to this community, focusing primarily on 1 John.

Sin in the Gospel According to John

The churches to which 1 John was written would have in their possession certain understandings of sin from the Gospel according to John. Several conclusions may be reached about sin from the Fourth Gospel.

1. It is clear that the world is guilty of sin and this sin must be removed by the sacrificial death of Jesus (1:29). This idea is supported by the fact that Jesus died on the cross at the very time the paschal lambs were killed (John 19:32-36).

2. Physical infirmity may sometimes be the direct result of sin, an implication of Jesus' words to the man healed at the Pool of Bethesda (5:14).[2] This causal relationship does not always exist, however (9:2, 3).

3. Those who reject the testimony of Jesus will die in their sin of unbelief (8:21, 24), but Jesus himself is without sin. In fact, those who reject Jesus' testimony believe that He is a sinner (9:16, 24, 31) and come to conclusions that are at odds with His own pro-

---

[2]Cf. J.C. Thomas, "Stop Sinning Lest Something Worse Come Upon You," *Journal for the Study of the New Testament* 59 (1995), pp. 3-20.

nouncements (9:34). This is in contrast to those who believe in Him (9:25).

4. Part of the Paraclete's ministry is to convict the world (prove it wrong) concerning sin (16:8, 9).

5. Jesus' words in 20:23 imply that believers play some role in the forgiveness of sins.

6. There are also several implicit statements about the forgiveness and/or the means of forgiveness of sins. In 13:1-20, footwashing was instituted as a sign of the continual cleansing available for postconversion sins. Jesus also assigned cleansing and sanctifying power to His word (15:3) and the Father's word (17:17).

The Life Setting of 1 John

Unlike 3 John, 1 and 2 John give evidence that the Johannine community was in an intense fight with a group of false teachers. John called these teachers deceivers and antichrists. Second John is clearly a quick letter dashed off by the Elder to warn a church at some distance of the impending visit of the false teachers. It appears to have been written shortly after their emergence.

In contrast, 1 John suggests that some time had transpired since the first appearance of the deceivers. This is based in part on the fact that by the time 1 John was written, the false teachers had left the Johannine community (2:18-27; 4:1-6). Apparently they had established an alternative community with its own distinctive interpretation of the Johannine teaching about Jesus. But before these opponents left the Johannine community, they caused such serious problems that a more comprehensive response was needed than was given in 2 John 10, 11. In that letter he admonished them not to aid or abet these false teachers.

It appears that 1 John represents the result of the theological reflection generated within the community over the teaching of the opponents. This document, then, was written to encourage those within the community to remain loyal to "that which was received from the beginning" (1:1). In doing so, it responded to the views of the opponents who wished to lead the faithful astray.[3] From the strategic appearance of the words "eternal life" in the book (1:2; 2:25; 3:15; 5:11-13, 20), it appears the author was concerned that the false teaching could jeopardize his readers' salvation.[4] Clearly then, 1 John was addressed to believers. With this bit of Johannine background, we will now examine three texts in 1 John which relate to our topic.

1 John 1:5—2:6

Verse 5 introduces one of the major themes of 1 John. In it we are told that God is light and that there is no darkness in Him at all. This statement serves to prepare the reader for a discussion emphasizing the necessity of moral purity. Unfortunately, the next portion of the text is a bit difficult to interpret because the author appears to be responding to the false teaching of the deceivers. It is not altogether clear exactly what

---

[3]For a more detailed study of the life setting, see J.C. Thomas "The Order of the Composition of the Johannine Epistles," *Novum Testamentum* 37 (1995), pp. 68-75.

[4]Since 1 John shares few of the characteristics of letters from the first century, many scholars view it as a kind of sermon. Closer examination reveals that it functions as a commentary of sorts upon the Gospel of John. It is not a commentary in the traditional sense but rather one which seeks to address the specific portions of the Fourth Gospel that the deceivers were distorting.

the deceivers' beliefs were. What *is* clear is that the false teachers did not have the appropriate attitude toward sin and its consequences. The entire section deals in one way or another with the issue of sin.

In the first part of the passage, John used three erroneous claims, which no doubt came from the deceivers themselves, to address the problem of sin for the community. The focus of the first claim is the issue of fellowship with God. The Greek term for *fellowship* (κοινωνία) occurs previously in the prologue of 1 John 1:3, and is identified as the purpose of John's proclamation to his readers. In that context it signifies a solidarity of belief in what "was from the beginning" and results in a deep unity with both the Father and the Son.

In 2 John 11, the Elder warned the congregation that if they received deceivers who were not confessing "Jesus Christ coming in the flesh" (v. 7), they fellowshipped or shared in the deceivers' evil works. Therefore for John, fellowship could be understood in both a positive and negative sense. Apparently, the deceivers were claiming fellowship with God but denied that this relationship had any connection with moral behavior. But as John's response points out, it is impossible to be in relationship with God if one's moral actions are at odds with God's character. A claim (or a lifestyle which claims) that one's actions are unrelated to one's relationship with God is patently false and, therefore, far from doing the truth.

In contrast to this erroneous claim of the false teachers, the author upheld the practice of walking in the light. "To walk" is a familiar metaphor in the Johannine Epistles, occurring here and in 1 John 2:11; 2 John 4, 6; and 3 John 3, 4. Three ideas are present in its use:

First, in the context of 1 John walking is tied to fellowship both positively (1:7) and negatively (v. 6). "To walk" is paramount to "having fellowship with."

Second, walking in truth is to live according to the commands of God/Jesus (2 John 6).

Third, since the greatest command in the Johannine community was to love one another (1 John 3:11), one's love toward the brothers was a sign one was walking in the truth. It is impossible to walk in the truth if one hates a brother (1 John 2:11). An example of how these ideas come together is found in 3 John 3, 4. There, the Elder stated that when Gaius walked in the truth he was acknowledging that he had fellowship with Jesus. This is evidenced by the fact that he loved the brothers, which he proved by his generous hospitality toward them. Therefore, to use the idea of walking in the light here in 1 John 1:7 is to emphasize the right conduct of the believers.

Two things may be deduced about one who walks in the light. First, this believer has fellowship. Oddly, John did not say here that this fellowship is with God; rather, John said that the fellowship is with one another. Such an unexpected shift underscores the fact that for John salvation is not an individualistic, pietistic experience, but must be rooted and grounded in community. For John, one's walking in the light can be judged on the basis of one's relationships in the community of faith. A second deduction made about those who walk in the light is that "the blood of Jesus . . . cleanses us from all sin." Such a statement makes it clear that the basis of one's forgiveness is the atoning death of Jesus, "the Lamb of God, who takes away the sin of the world" (John 1:29).

This talk of sin leads to two false claims: "If we claim

to be without sin" (1 John 1:8) and "If we claim we have not sinned" (v. 10). The precise meaning of these claims is a bit uncertain. It is not altogether clear whether the deceivers were claiming they had always been completely free from sin, as later Gnostics thought, or if they were claiming that on the basis of their relationship to Jesus they were free from sin permanently. The latter interpretation is more likely, for John quickly made clear that believers can (and do!) sin. A few observations are offered about these claims and John's evaluation of them. The author clearly denounced such boasts as deception (or lies) and made it explicit that this position is far from God's truth, or Word. In addition to the general truth contained in his words of reply, it is interesting that each of John's responses closely parallel one another in form. Rather than denying the presence of sin, John advocated the confession of sin for the purpose of forgiveness (v. 9). Three aspects of this verse deserve specific comment:

1. The verb *confess* (ὁμολογῶμεν) is in the present tense, not the past tense, which suggests that the confession John advocated is to be a continuing, regular part of the community's life, not a onetime occurrence.[5] It may be that this confession was a public one to others in the community.[6]

---

[5]Cf. especially the comments of C.H. Talbert, *Reading John: A Literary and Theological Commentary on the Fourth Gospel and the Johannine Epistles* (New York: Crossroads, 1992), p. 20: "'If we regularly confess [present tense] our sins [Proverbs 28:13], he is faithful and just [Deuteronomy 32:4; see also 1 Clement 27:1; 60:1], and will go on forgiving [present tense] our sins and cleansing us from all unrighteousness' (v. 9). Regular confession yields regular forgiveness of guilt and cleansing from the stain of sin."

[6]Cf. the discussion in R.E. Brown, *The Epistles of John* (Garden City, N.Y.: Doubleday, 1982), p. 208.

2. John seems to have gone out of his way to stress the willingness and ability of Jesus to grant forgiveness and bring cleansing from sin: "He is *faithful and just.*"

3. There is also an emphasis on the extent or completeness of the cleansing: "from *all* unrighteousness."

It could very well be that 1 John 2:1, 2 should be interpreted as standing with the statement found in 1:10, which immediately precedes it in the text.[7] In any case, lest his previous statements be misconstrued, John quickly revealed his intention that his readers avoid sin at all costs. Even though he desired moral perfection for his community, the author acknowledged the possibility of postconversion sin and the necessity of remedying it through the same means by which their conversion was accomplished, appropriating the effects of the atoning death of Jesus. In this passage John sought to emphasize both the need to remove postconversion sin and the means by which it is done.

In 2:3-6, John brought the argument back to where it began in 1:6, 7. At the same time, he revealed the rationale for the urgency of his message regarding sin. Keeping the commands, or walking in the light, is absolutely essential if our claims to know God are legitimate.

1 John 3:5-10

It seems odd that John would include a discussion about sin here that appears to be in such diametric opposition to what he wrote previously. In chapters 1

---

[7] In the original Greek text of 1 John there were no chapter, verse, sentence, or word divisions, so that for the original readers of this work, 2:1 would not be separated from 1:10 in any way.

and 2 the possibility of a believer sinning was all too real, but here such a state seems to be completely denied. What is to be made of such a tension? Do we simply have a contradiction in the book?[8] Two things must be kept in mind when approaching this passage:

First, John had earlier acknowledged the possibility that believers can (and do) commit sin. Whatever 3:5-10 means, it must fit within this broader Johannine framework.

Second, an understanding of the immediate context of this passage can help in its interpretation. In 1 John 2:28—3:3, the writer placed a great deal of emphasis upon the fact that his readers were children of God. In chapter 1, he stated that one's nature can be discerned by one's actions or life. Here, the one who is born of God is the one who does righteousness. John's readers are also admonished that in the light of the return of Jesus, they are to purify themselves just as He is pure.

Within the context of this discussion about the children of God—which concludes with a statement about sin—John offered additional comments about believers and sin in 3:5-10. The following outline of this passage may help reveal its major thrust:

I. Jesus was manifested to destroy sin, for He is sinless (v. 5).

  A. Each one who remains in Him does not sin (v. 6a).

  B. Each one who sins has not seen Him or known Him (v. 6b).

---

[8]The limitations of space prohibit an examination of the various theories put forward as a possible solution to this dilemma. For surveys of the various positions, see I de la Potterie, "L'impeccabilite du chretien d'apres I John 3, 6:9," *L'Evangile de Jean: Etudes et Problemes* (ed. F.M. Braun; Bruges, Belgium: Desclee De Brouwer, 1958), pp. 162-177, and S.S. Smalley, *1, 2, 3 John* (Waco: Word, 1984), pp. 159-63.

II. "Children, let no one deceive you" (v. 7a).
    A. The one who does what is right is righteous, just as He is (v. 7b).
    B. Each one who sins is of the devil; he sins from the beginning (v. 8a).
III. The Son of God was manifested to destroy the devil's work (v. 8b).
    A. Each one born of God does not commit sin (v. 9a) . . .
        1. Because His seed remains in him (v.9b).
        2. Because he is born of God (v. 9d).
    B. Children of God and children of the devil are manifested in this (v. 10a).
    C. Each one who does not do righteousness is not of God (v. 10b, c).

Clearly, John's main concern in this passage was to bring the children of God and the children of the devil into sharp contrast. The lines of demarcation should be obvious to all. If Jesus has come to destroy sin, then those who remain in Him do not sin. Conversely, those who commit sin show their true character. Apparently the deceivers were advocating that one's moral actions have nothing, or little, to do with one's relationship with God. John saw such an attitude as so dangerous that this strong warning was needed. There is no middle ground—one's actions reveal one's nature. Sin is of the devil; righteousness is from God! How odd such simplistic language sounds—odd until one begins to reflect on the contemporary situation in the "Christian world."

Still, John's strong words in verse 9, that a believer is not able to sin, are difficult to reconcile with his previous and later statements about the possibility of a believer sinning. One attractive solution to this problem, which has some grammatical support, is to emphasize the point that in this passage the Greek verb for sin (ἁμαρτάνω) always appears in the present tense. In this interpretation John was saying that one born of God does not sin habitually, as a course of habit, but rather occasionally sins. In other words, while there is the possibility of a Christian sinning, there is no possibility of a sinning Christian.

This interpretation is appealing, because it seems to fit so well with our experience as believers. It may indeed be what John meant. Yet such an interpretation does not seem to do justice to the vigor and intensity of John's words. In some ways it pulls the teeth from John's language and suggests that sin in the life of the believer is not *that* unusual. So perhaps we should stay with this text just a little longer before settling on an interpretation.

As John Wesley suggested long ago (Sermon 15), perhaps the key to understanding this passage is the word *remain/abide* (μένω). It occurs twice in this text: In verse 6, "Each one who remains in Him does not sin," and in verse 9, "Each one born of God does not sin, because His seed [σπέρμα] remains in him." Wesley believed that while it was possible for those born again to commit outward sin, outward sin was the result of a process which comes dangerously close to the loss of one's faith. He explains:

> He fell, step by step, first, into negative, inward sin, not "stirring up the gift of God which was in him," not "watching unto prayer," not "pressing on to the mark of the prize of his high calling": then

into positive inward sin, inclining to wickedness with his heart, giving way to some evil desire or temper: next he lost his faith, his sight of a pardoning God, and consequently his love of God; and, being then weak and like another man, he was capable of committing even outward sin.[9]

While Wesley may overstate the case, in the light of 1 John 1 and 2—a testimony to the fact that a believer might sin, not testimony of a backslidden believer—his interpretation does preserve the force and power of John's words. Specifically, one who sins is siding with the devil and chooses not to remain in Jesus. Sin, then, is not inconsequential but disrupts one's relationship with God, which can lead to complete estrangement. At what point the seed of God ceases to abide in the believer is difficult to determine. Thankfully, God himself knows. However, let us not lose sight of the fact that the point of this passage is to remind believers that sin ultimately leads to the devil and must be avoided at all costs. Perhaps the tension between chapters 1 and 2 and chapter 3 was intended by John to ensure that his readers did not become complacent about sin but would take a no-nonsense approach to this pivotal issue.

1 John 5:16-18

A final text in 1 John dealing with sin is no less enigmatic than the one just examined. It has been the subject of intense investigation and speculation:

If anyone sees his brother sinning a sin not unto death, he should ask [pray] and he will give him

---

[9]John Wesley, *The Works of Wesley: Sermons I* (ed. E.H. Sugden; Grand Rapids: Francis Asbury Press), pp. 307-308.

life, to those who sin not unto death. There is a
sin unto death. Not concerning that one do I say
you should ask [pray]. All wrongdoing is sin, and
there is sin not unto death. We know that each
one born of God does not sin, but the one born of
God keeps him and the evil one cannot touch him.

A number of questions rise naturally from this text.
What is the "sin unto death"? Can the prayer of a
believer actually result in life for one who sins? Who is
it that gives this life? Are believers not to pray for those
who have sinned unto death? Who is this one born of
God who keeps the believer beyond the reach of the
Evil One? Is it Jesus or (the prayers of) another believer? Questions such as these are fascinating, but they
often lead interpreters far from the central thrust of
John's argument. Although we will address several of
these issues, for our purposes it is most important to
identify John's primary point in this passage.

In the text that immediately precedes this one, the
author stated that believers can have the confidence
to ask for anything in accordance with the will of the
Father and know that they will receive the things for
which they ask. This admonition, no doubt, is based
on the words of Jesus in the Fourth Gospel (14:13,
14; 15:16; 16:23, 24), and was probably appealed to
in a variety of situations to encourage the community
to pray.

In 1 John 5:15-18, John moved from this word of
general exhortation to a specific situation where
believers are encouraged to pray when they see a
brother or sister sin (a sin unto death). It is not altogether clear what John meant when he said to "see" a
brother sin, but it is obvious what one is to do: inter-

cede in prayer.[10] Although God is more than likely the One who gives life, since this is John's view in the rest of the Johannine writings, the Greek text implies that the one who prays gives life to the one who has sinned. Such an assertion, when taken with the statement in John 20:23 and the fellow believer's reconciliatory role in footwashing, suggests that Christians are to take an aggressively active role in ministry to brothers and sisters who have sinned. John was consistent in emphasizing that believers are morally accountable for the spiritual welfare of their brothers and sisters.[11]

The warning that there is a sin unto death underscores the gravity of the presence of sin in the believer's life. Whatever the precise meaning of this phrase,[12] it underscores the possibility that a member of the community could forfeit his or her salvation. John stressed the dire consequences of this sin by stating that this is not the sin for which he advocated intercession. Does this imply that a believer is not to pray for one who commits a sin unto death? John reminds the reader that all wrongdoing is sin, while reaffirming the truth that

---

[10]The idea of intercession for sinners would be familiar to the readers from the Old Testament. For examples, cf. R. Schnackenburg, *The Johannine Epistles* (tr. R. and S. Fuller; New York: Crossroads, 1992), pp. 248, 49, and I.H. Marshall, *The Epistles of John* (Grand Rapids: Eerdmans, 1978), p. 246, note 16.

[11]A similar idea is found in James 5:16. Cf. chapter 9.

[12]Proposals include (a) intentional sin as opposed to unintentional, as described in the Old Testament and the Dead Sea Scrolls; (b) the blasphemy against the Spirit, of which Jesus spoke; (c) the sin of the unrepentant, sexually immoral person in the church at Corinth, for whom Paul recommended expulsion; (d) the apostasy of which the Book of Hebrews speaks; and (e) the later mortal as opposed to venial sins which the church eventually identified. Whatever the precise identification of this sin, it would appear that those guilty would now be outside the Johannine community. See also the discussion in D.M. Smith, *First, Second, and Third John* (Louisville: John Knox, 1991), pp. 133, 34.

those born of God do not sin.

This line of thought is brought to a close in verse 18 by noting that "the one . . . born of God keeps him." This phrase is open to at least three interpretations:

1. It is possible to take "the one . . . born of God keeps him" as referring to Jesus, although oddly enough 1 John does not use that exact description for Jesus.

2. It is possible to take the phrase to mean that a believer can keep a brother or sister (through prayer)!

3. Some manuscripts read "keeps himself" rather than "keeps him." Thus, the phrase could be a call to self-vigilance on the part of the believer to remain in Jesus.

At any rate, this verse reinforces the fact that sin is a serious matter for the believer and must be opposed at every point.

Conclusion

What is one to conclude from this brief study of sin in 1 John, and what are the implications of these conclusions for the Church of God?

1. *It is clear that the Johannine community struggled with postconversion sin.* The presence of sin was neither denied nor ignored.

2. *John's response to the presence of sin was to insist that the believer appropriate the sacrificial blood of Jesus to bring cleansing.* Confession was the primary means by which such appropriation was made.

3. *John's method of dealing with sin was remarkably communal.* Not only does it appear that public confession was part of the community's practice, but it is also the case that individual believers had a moral obliga-

tion to look out for one another spiritually.

4. *Sin was such a serious issue that it could lead to the loss of salvation.* This meant that there was no lackadaisical attitude to sin for the Johannine community.

What does all of this mean for the Church of God? More pointedly, what concrete changes might be made on the basis of what has been discovered regarding sin from 1 John to prevent the spiritual failure of leaders? While it might seem presumptuous for me to offer advice on such matters, for integrity's sake it seems that I should at least have to attempt a response to the issues which I raised at the beginning of this chapter. So if the following remarks seem wild, strange, or impractical, just attribute them to a younger brother who still has a way to go before reaching maturity.

First and most importantly, we must devise ways to make accountability a regular and meaningful part of our lives as Christian leaders. This means that spiritual oversight and nurture must become an active, integral part of our "job descriptions" as leaders. What may be the most discouraging aspect of this challenge is that one person is hard-pressed to offer such care to more than 10-15 people. When fewer people are involved, there is the temptation to reduce the covenant to a private contract between individuals, a practice that some in the church seem to have perfected into an art! When more people are involved there is the temptation to hide and conceal, rather than participate and reveal.

But nurturing and pastoral care take time, with regular and consistent periods for reflection and fellowship. So how can the church begin to provide such nurture and pastoral care for its leaders? The natural place to begin is with the district overseer, a largely underutilized and ignored resource in our church. What would happen if the church trained and charged these pastors with the spiritual oversight of the pastors on their district, if we moved from a strategy of program caretakers to pastoral caregivers? One such attempt could be to meet together once or twice a month for a time of reflection as a group in which our pastors would agree to submit to one another and to support one another for the perfecting of the saints. This would free the state overseer and his associates to offer the same kind of regular pastoral care to groups of district overseers. In turn, our general overseer and his assistants could arrange for regular meetings with groups of state overseers. Sure it would take time and money. But do we not regularly spend time and money on ventures far less worthy than the pastoral care of our leaders? We simply cannot afford to allow everyone to do right in his own eyes. Such behavior leads to disastrous results.

Second, we must somehow reconnect with the local church in ways that have integrity these leaders who have become disconnected from the local church. In other words, we must commit to making leaders more than just guests in their "home church." In this scenario, pastors would be charged with helping these "parishioners" with issues like distribution of time, motives for travel, and a balance in personal and family matters, issues that are seldom reviewed with anyone.

Third, if the kinds of accountability suggested above are implemented, some of our problems with the sins of worldly success, political ambition, greed, and pride will begin to be addressed as believers speak the truth in love to another about these areas of our lives. But in addition, perhaps the time has come for radical, prophetic action in the realm of politics, money, and pride.

What if the church truly rejected the corporate business executive model of church leadership (and its trappings), replacing it with one which resembles New Testament models more closely? What if a congregation, department, school, state, or region decided to pay each of its ministers, administrators, and /or faculty members the same remuneration, as a protest against the world's method of valuation? What would happen if we brought our political process out into the open and those interested in serving the church in a specific capacity could campaign for that post, instead of the covert campaigning that now takes place? Or, what if we discarded our overly politicized system altogether and waited until the Lord of Glory came among us and spoke to us establishing his own *Pentecostal* polity?

The ravings of a lunatic you say? Or simply the ramblings of a misguided scholar who is a bit out of his depth in such matters? Maybe! Or it is just the heartfelt passion of one of your sons, longing for the kingdom of God to be on earth as it is in heaven. These are perilous times. Smoke and mirrors will not do.

I close with a quote from our grandfather, John Wesley:

> Let us learn, lastly, to follow that direction of the great Apostle, "Be not high-minded, but fear." Let us fear sin more than death or hell. Let us have a jealous (though not painful) fear, lest we should lean to our own deceitful hearts. "Let him that standeth take

heed lest he fall." Even he who now standeth fast in the grace of God, in the faith that overcometh the world, may nevertheless fall into inward sin, and thereby "make shipwreck of his faith." And how easily then will outward sin regain its dominion over him! Thou, therefore, O man of God! watch always, that thou mayest always hear the voice of God! Watch, that thou mayest pray without ceasing, at all times, and in all places, pouring out thy heart before Him! So shalt thou always believe, and always love, and never commit sin.[13]

---

[13]Wesley, *The Works of Wesley: Sermons I*, p. 312.

MINISTERING THE SACRAMENTS

This study, which focuses on the sacraments or ordinances of the church, is divided into four major parts. The initial section will seek to define the term *sacrament*, briefly survey the various ways in which sacraments are thought to function, and list the practices which the Church of God designates as sacraments. The next three parts of the study investigate the biblical basis for each of these practices individually, discuss their theological significance, and offer some reflection on their practice and administration in contemporary worship. The chapter concludes with a suggested order of worship for Footwashing and Lord's Supper.

Various churches have different ideas about the

number of sacraments and the way in which they function. In the history of the church the sacraments have been seen as remembrances of what Jesus has done, as symbols of a spiritual reality but not the reality itself, as signs of a spiritual reality which identify with that reality in a substantive way, as acts which actually convey grace, or as mechanical rites in which grace is dispensed somewhat magically. Despite such a wide divergence in views, each of these positions grows out of attempts to understand how these acts function in the church. Rather than examine each of these theories in detail, it would be better to bring clarity to this topic as we examine the biblical basis for each of these practices.

While the number of sacraments recognized by various churches ranges from two to seven, the Church of God, along with several other churches, recognizes three practices as falling within this classification. These are Water Baptism, Footwashing (or Washing the Saints' Feet), and the Lord's Supper (also called the Communion and the Eucharist). Each of these practices will receive individual attention in the following sections.

Water Baptism

The Biblical Basis for Water Baptism

The origin of the practice of water baptism can be traced to the ministry of John the Baptist. This prophetic figure appeared, preaching a conversion baptism for the forgiveness of sins. Response to his message required confession of sin before God and the participation of baptism at John's hand. Some have sought to understand John's baptism against the backdrop of proselyte baptism or the washings that took place at Qumran. In contrast to proselyte baptism, however, John's baptism signified the forgiveness of sin. In contrast to Qumran, it was a onetime, unrepeatable act that was open to all who would repent. Therefore, John's baptism was a unique action in the first century A.D.

In coming to John for baptism, Jesus acknowledged the legitimacy of John's baptism and identified with his ministry. Although He had no need for forgiveness of sin, Jesus stood solid with His people as their Messiah by undergoing a conversion baptism. In addition to submitting to the baptism of John, Jesus and/or His disciples baptized believers during Jesus' earthly ministry (John 3:22; 4:1, 2). Apparently this baptism, like John's, was a sign of forgiveness. It is difficult to avoid the conclusion that these baptismal activities were closely connected to John's own.

Not only did Jesus receive and administer water baptism, but He also specifically commanded His disciples (followers) to go into all the world, making disciples of all nations, baptizing them in the name of the Father, Son, and Holy Spirit (Matthew 28:19).

This foundation and command explains Peter's admonitions in his Pentecost sermon for his hearers to repent and be baptized (Acts 2:38). About 3,000 accepted his message and were baptized (v. 41). The Book of Acts documents the baptism of a number of others. These include the Samaritans (8:12) and the Ethiopian Eunuch (8:36-38), both baptized by Philip; Paul (9:18), who was baptized by Ananias; Cornelius and his household (10:47, 48), who were baptized by Peter; Lydia (16:14, 15), the Philippian jailer and his household (16:33), Crispus (18:8), and the disciples in Ephesus (19:5), all baptized by Paul. In 1 Corinthians 1:14, 16, Paul acknowledged that he baptized Crispus and Gaius and the household of Stephanas.

Other New Testament texts imply baptism was practiced in the early church, as well as a number of references in early Christian writings that are not part of the New Testament itself.

The Theological Significance of Water Baptism

According to the New Testament there are several ways in which water baptism is theologically significant.

1. Water baptism is a sign of the complete cleansing from sin that one experiences in conversion. Such an understanding is certainly present in the preaching of John and Peter about baptism, and it is probable that this was the view of Jesus as well. This understanding is not unrelated to the way in which baptism functions as a sign of regeneration (Titus 3:5).

2. Baptism is a sign of entering into the death and resurrection of Jesus by entering into the watery grave and being resurrected unto eternal life. The connection between baptism and the death of Jesus is present in Mark 10:38; Romans 6:3,4; and Colossians 2:12.

3. This rite is also a sign of the believer's incorporation into the body of Christ, as Paul made clear in 1 Corinthians 12:13 and Galatians 3:27. As such it is a sign of the believer's public proclamation of faith and is also a sign that the church places its seal of acceptance upon this believer.

Given the theological significance of water baptism, when the baptism of converts is undertaken by the church, it is a most important function.

Specific Issues Pertaining to Water Baptism

After a survey of the biblical basis for and the theological significance of water baptism, we are now in a position to address several important issues related to the ministering of this practice.

The Agent of Water Baptism. Nothing in the New Testament suggests that the oversight of the practice of baptism was restricted to a specific group of people (i.e., the clergy). There is, therefore, nothing in the biblical text itself that prohibits any believer from baptizing a convert in water. In fact, Paul indicated that he rarely baptized his converts but left that aspect of ministry to others. Nor is there biblical justification for the exclusion of female believers from this ministry of the church. Consequently, any reluctance on the part of the church regarding the involvement of women in this function in principle has no biblical grounds.

The Church of God, as most denominations, has sought to restrict those who perform water baptism to those whom the church recognizes as qualified leaders, in order to protect the practice from abuse and to ensure its proper observance. Such a move is understandable, but it is clearly not a decision based on biblical precedent. In this regard, the recent move by the Church of God to recognize the qualification of women ministers for this ministry is a step toward a more biblical position. To state the obvious, women ministers are fully qualified to participate as agents in the practice of water baptism.

The Mode of Water Baptism. Although the mode of baptism in a number of denominations is sprinkling or pouring of water on the head of the person receiving baptism, the Church of God, with many other churches, practices baptism by immersion. There are several reasons for this decision regarding mode.

1. It seems to be in keeping with the meaning of the Greek word (βαπτίζω), which means "to dip" or "plunge."

2. Immersion is a better symbol for the many things which baptism represents: complete cleansing; identification with the death, burial, and resurrection of Jesus; and incorporation into the new reality of the body of Christ.

3. The earliest records of water baptism outside the New Testament in the early church indicate that immersion was the preferred method (see *Didache* 7:1-3).[1]

The Formula. What are the words to be said just before the person is baptized? Two formulas appear to have been used in the early church. Several texts in the New Testament suggest that a number of believers were baptized "in the name of Jesus." Such a formula must be understood in its first-century context. To baptize one in Jesus' name at this time was to make clear to all those around that this was a Christian baptism and that one was being baptized into Jesus as Savior. Theoretically, baptism in the name of Jesus is a legitimate formula of baptism as practiced in the New Testament.

The situation today is somewhat different in that there are those who demand baptism in Jesus' name as the only acceptable formula. At stake is the theo-

---

[1] In order to preserve the symbolism of baptism, it is important that the candidate for baptism be completely submerged under the water. It is appropriate to have more than one person participate as agents in this practice.

logical understanding of God's unity and diversity. Baptism in Jesus' name is often an attempt to place emphasis on the oneness of God (one person rather than three) and, in so doing, exclude a trinitarian understanding of God.

The Church of God baptizes "in the name of the Father and of the Son and of the Holy Spirit." The primary reason for this practice is that this is the formula Jesus instructed His disciples to use in Matthew 28:19. Attempts to interpret the name in this passage as Jesus are an intrusion in the Matthean text. In addition to following the command of Jesus, the Matthean baptismal formula places a special emphasis on the worship of God in His fullness as Father, Son, and Holy Spirit.

Should water baptism ever be repeated? From all the available evidence it would appear that baptism is to be a once-for-all act. Ordinarily, to repeat baptism is to treat it in a cavalier fashion and exhibits a misunderstanding of its significance. However, there are at least two reasons for rebaptism: (1) if the first baptism was invalid because of mode, formula, or state of the heart; (2) if one goes back into open sin.

Two things can help prevent invalid rebaptisms: (1) the reliving of one's own baptism when a brother or sister is being baptized and (2) a proper understanding of footwashing.

Suggested Elements of a Baptismal Service:
1. It is important for baptism to be treated as part of the church's normal worship, not as an add-on or a nonessential part.
2. A short homily should be offered just before or during the baptismal portion of the service, reminding

the congregation and the baptismal candidates of the significance of this event.

3. The community aspect of this practice should be emphasized. This includes things like architecture. Unfortunately, most churches have a baptistry that is as far removed as possible from the congregation, creating an unnecessary separation and turning the congregation into spectators. Invite the congregation as close as possible to the baptismal site.

4. It is important to allow the convert an opportunity to give a word of testimony regarding his/her faith. It is also appropriate to call on another individual or two for testimonies who have a special interest in the person being baptized.

5. Offer a prayer for the candidate (or have someone else in the congregation offer a prayer).

6. Speak the baptismal formula—something like, "By the authority vested in me as a licensed/ordained minister in the Church of God, I baptize this my brother/sister in the name of the Father and of the Son and of the Holy Spirit."

7. Quietly inform the candidate that he or she may hold his/her nose if he/she wishes. Being immersed in water can be a traumatic experience for some individuals.

8. Have the candidates to hold their hands at their chest. Then place one hand behind the head and one hand on their hands and immerse them in water. Tell them beforehand to allow you to immerse them completely and to pull them up. If you have to baptize a large number of people, or if you need assistance with particularly tall or heavy people, arrange for someone to assist you in the water.

9. It is wise to have someone assist those baptized as they come up out of the baptistry.

10. Appropriate music before, during, and after the baptismal portion of the service is always in order.

11. While it is proper for you to baptize in ordinary church clothes, baptismal robes are available at many religious bookstores.

Footwashing

In addition to water baptism, the Church of God recognizes another rite of cleansing that is repeatable in nature and, as such, is a part of the church's continuing ministry. While many denominations do not recognize Footwashing as a sacrament, a remarkably large number of churches do assign it sacramental status.

The Biblical Basis for Footwashing

Two New Testament texts support the practice of Footwashing as a sacrament. The primary passage is found in John 13:1-20. In this text, shortly before His betrayal and death, Jesus rose from the Passover meal, laid aside His garments, poured water into a basin, and began to wash the feet of His disciples. After He completed this washing, He put His clothes back on and reclined with the disciples once again. At this point in the story Jesus commanded the disciples to wash one another's feet.

Since there is some controversy about whether footwashing is to be a sacrament, specific attention should be given to its institution. *First, as with baptism, we have the example of Jesus to follow.* His action is unparalleled in antiquity, for there is no evidence in any ancient literature that a superior voluntarily washed the feet of a subordinate. Such an example is surely worthy of emulation. *Second, added to the weight of this example are the commands of Jesus to continue the practice.* In contrast to the single commands to baptize and celebrate the Lord's Supper, there are three commands to practice footwashing:

1. In verse 14, Jesus made it explicit that the disciples were to wash one another's feet. In the light of its other uses in the writings of John (John 19:7; 1 John 2:6; 3:16; 4:11; 3 John 8), the Greek word translated "ought" (ὀφείλω) should be understood in the sense of obligation, rather than in the sense of a good idea. In other words, verse 14 shows that Jesus was requiring this action, not suggesting it.

2. In verse 15, Jesus said that He had given them an example. Careful attention should be given to the Greek word translated "example" (ὑπόδειγμα). In ancient Greek medical manuals, this term was used for an illustration or picture, showing how to do surgery, etc. Perhaps a better translation would be "prototype." The disciples were to do just as Jesus had done.

3. Verse 17 pronounces a blessing on those who not only know these things but do them. One is hard-pressed to know how else Jesus could have instituted this practice, if not in using the words He did.

The other biblical text that shows footwashing being practiced in the early church comes from 1 Timothy 5:10, where in order for a widow to be supported by the church, she must have "washed the feet of the saints."

The Theological Significance of Footwashing

In order to understand the theological significance of footwashing, careful attention must be paid to John

13:10. Earlier in the passage Jesus made clear to Peter that the washing was no mere gesture of hospitality but had eternal consequences (vv. 6-8). In verse 10 He explained the meaning of footwashing: "The one who has been bathed has no need to wash except the feet, but is wholly clean."

In the ancient world when a host would invite a guest to a banquet, the guest would bathe at home. When he/she arrived at the host's house, water would be provided to wash the feet in order to remove the dust that had accumulated on the journey. Another bath was not required. Jesus has taken the analogy of the ancient banquet and turned it into a religious practice. In this sense the one who has bathed is the one who has been baptized. Such a one has no need of rebaptism but only the footwashing. The footwashing, then, is a sign of the continual cleansing available to the believer. In that sense it functions as an extension of baptism—just as baptism was the sign of complete cleansing, footwashing is the sign of continual cleansing.

When the church gathers to wash one another's feet, the individual believer both renders and receives this ministry while being obedient to the commands of the Lord. Because of its significance, footwashing services are an important part of the church's ministry and are wonderful opportunities for reconciliation between brothers and sisters. If footwashing is a sign of forgiveness of sin, then footwashing is rooted in the atoning death of Jesus. While the issue of humble service is clearly present, it is secondary to the theme of cleansing.

Specific Issues Pertaining to Footwashing

The Minister of Footwashing. The biblical texts suggest that everyone is to participate in this practice. The clearest biblical evidence regarding those involved in the observance shows that women were involved. Therefore, it would seem that any believer could lead in this worship, although the Church of God has placed this responsibility primarily in the hands of the clergy.

The Frequency. Ideally, footwashing should accompany the observance of the Lord's Supper, as it is a wonderful preparation for this celebration. Given its theological significance, this opportunity should be made available throughout the year. Perhaps a quarterly observance would be a good beginning point.

Appropriate Contexts for Footwashing. Footwashing fits well within the context of the community's worship and serves well just before the Lord's Supper. It can, however, be observed on its own in other contexts: in small groups, hospital visitation, as a sign of closure in specific kinds of counseling, as part of marriage seminars, in preparation for revival, for purposes of reconciliation with a brother or sister, and many other occasions.

Suggested Elements:

1. It is important for footwashing to be treated as part of the church's normal worship, not as an add-on or a nonessential part.

2. A short homily should be offered just before the footwashing portion of the service, reminding the congregation of the significance of this event. This should include the reading of a text relevant to the occasion.

3. The community aspect of this practice should be emphasized. While issues of modesty should be kept

in mind, there are no biblical grounds for separating men and women. Such separation can be taken as a sign of division in the body.

4. Enough basins of water and towels should be present for every two participants to have access to one.

5. Given the theological significance of footwashing, encourage those in need of reconciliation to wash one another's feet.

6. While rendering or receiving the washing, pray and reflect on the ways in which God has forgiven you and your brother/sister, and pray for God's purification in your life.

7. Allow testimonies during this service.

8. Appropriate music before, during, and after the footwashing is always in order.

A final word should perhaps be said about the reinstitution of footwashing in churches where it has been discontinued. Perhaps a couple of annual community celebrations should be encouraged: during the week of Easter (Thursday preceding) and at another appropriate time (perhaps New Year's Eve). Occasionally, it might be possible to have several brothers or sisters wash one another's feet before the whole congregation as an act that precedes the Lord's Supper. This representative footwashing could function as a sign of the Lord's cleansing work and as an encouragement to others to participate in this practice. Encourage the various small groups in the church to observe this practice once or twice throughout the year.

The Lord's Supper

The sacrament of the Lord's Supper is also known as Communion and the Eucharist (a term which comes from the Greek word meaning "to give thanks"). The Roman Catholic Church believes that in the Eucharist the bread literally becomes the flesh of Jesus and the wine becomes His literal blood. This belief is called transubstantiationism. Lutherans, while denying that the elements become the literal body and blood of Jesus, believe that the real presence of Christ is in the elements. This belief is called consubstantiationism. Most Protestants believe that the elements are signs, or symbols, of the body and blood of Jesus.

The Biblical Basis for the Lord's Supper

The biblical evidence for the practice of the Lord's Supper is found in the synoptic Gospels (Matthew 26:26-30; Mark 14:22-26; Luke 22:15-20) and in the writings of Paul (1 Corinthians 11:23-26). Each of these texts describes the events of Jesus' last meal with His disciples in which He commanded them to continue the practice. Specifically, Jesus instructed the disciples to drink the fruit of the vine, which represents His blood, and to eat the bread, which represents His body. "Do this in remembrance of me," He said.

Other New Testament texts which may have reference to the meaning or the observance of the Lord's Supper include John 6:22-59 and the texts in Acts which make reference to the "breaking of bread" (2:42, 46; 20:7; 27:35, 36; see also 1 Corinthians 10:1-22; 11:17-22, 27-34; and Jude 12). A great deal of evidence exists in other early Christian literature that the Lord's Supper was a regular part of the church's worship.

The Theological Significance of the Lord's Supper

A number of important theological issues are signified in the Lord's Supper.

1. Since the Lord's Supper was instituted in the context of the Passover Feast, and since Jesus became the true Passover Lamb, the Lord's Supper serves to remind the believers of God's miraculous deliverance of Israel out of Egypt and the way in which the Passover anticipated the actions of the Lord on the night before His death.

2. The Lord's Supper was instituted in the context of the final meal which Jesus shared with His disciples after nearly three years of intimate fellowship. As such, the Lord's Supper serves as a reminder of that last meal.

3. Perhaps the most important aspect of the Lord's Supper is the way in which it reminds the worshipers of Jesus' death for our salvation. The imagery of the bread broken and the wine poured out graphically illustrates the death of Jesus.

4. The Lord's Supper is a visible sign of the spiritual nourishment which the believer receives from Christ. While such nourishment is received in a variety of ways in the Christian's life, the Lord's Supper is an especially appropriate opportunity for such engaging enrichment with our Lord.

5. The Lord's Supper is a sign of communion between the Lord and His church (He serves at the table), the communion of the believer and his/her Lord (the spiritual partaking of Christ), and the communion between the believer and other believers (the believers together form one body, or one loaf).

6. The Lord's Supper is an anticipation of the mes-

sianic meal that will one day be shared with Jesus in heaven. This is hinted at in Jesus' words at the Last Supper (Matthew 26:29; Luke 22:16, 18), in Paul's words in 1 Corinthians 11:26, and is made explicit in John's words in Revelation 19:7, 9 concerning the Marriage Supper of the Lamb.

Specific Issues Pertaining to the Lord's Supper

As with water baptism and footwashing, there are additional points that should be made regarding the practice of this sacrament.

The Minister. Except for the account of the Last Supper, the New Testament is strangely silent regarding who may lead in the celebration of the Lord's Supper. Therefore, there are no biblical grounds for restricting the administration of the Lord's Supper to the clergy. As with water baptism, the Church of God has placed the responsibility for leadership of the celebration of the Lord's Supper in the hands of the clergy. The rationale appears to be to protect the sanctity of the rite and ensure that it is not abused. Again, the move to allow women ministers to lead in the celebration of this sacrament is a move in a more biblical direction.

The Frequency. In early Christian practice, the Lord's Supper was celebrated quite frequently. There is some reason to believe that some early Christians celebrated the Lord's Supper each time they gathered together. All of this suggests that the Lord's Supper should be a regular part of our worship services. Although the Church of God has suggested that the Lord's Supper be celebrated at least quarterly, given the importance of this practice, perhaps a monthly celebration would be a good goal to set, although more frequent celebrations are certainly in order.

The Participants. The primary qualification for participation in the Lord's Supper is faith in Jesus Christ as Lord and Savior. Therefore, participation in the Lord's Supper should be open to any believer, regardless of denominational background. Only in extraordinarily extreme situations should an individual be denied access to the Lord's Supper, as when a member of the body has been excluded from the church on the order of 1 Corinthians 5:11 and Matthew 18:17.

Despite the fact that Paul gave a stern admonition about the need for self-examination before approaching the Table of the Lord, he did not direct the Corinthian believers to withdraw from the Table but to examine themselves. The implication is that the believer would rectify any problem during this period. Such times should not only encourage introspection but reconciliation in the body. Footwashing provides the perfect opportunity for such examination when it is observed prior to the celebration of the Lord's Supper.

Suggested Elements:

1. It is important for the Lord's Supper to be treated as part of the church's normal worship, not as an add-on or a nonessential part.

2. A short homily should be offered just before or during the Lord's Supper portion of the service, reminding the congregation of the significance of this event. This should include the reading of one of the texts which deal with the institution of the Lord's Supper.

3. The community aspect of this practice should be emphasized. Ideally, this would involve all the members of the congregation around a single table, with

one loaf and one cup. If this is a practical impossibility, measures should be taken to preserve as much of this community emphasis as possible. For example, perhaps several loaves could be used so that members of the congregation could take a piece from a loaf. Perhaps a symbolic pouring of the wine could take place in the sight of the church. If this proves impossible, wafers are available at many Christian bookstores.

4. A time of self-examination should be provided before the distribution of the elements.

5. Select men and women in the church beforehand to help in the distribution of the elements.

6. Before eating the bread, a prayer of thanksgiving and blessing should be offered by a member of the body. Then the leader should say, "The body of Christ broken for you." The same should be done for the cup, this time accompanied by, "The blood of Christ poured out for you."

7. A time of thanksgiving and praise should follow the eating of the bread and drinking of the cup.

8. Appropriate music before, during, and after the celebration of the Lord's Supper is always in order.

9. When the Lord's Supper is taken to those unable to attend the church service, a member of the body should accompany the minister in order to preserve the community aspect of the practice.

A Suggested Order of Worship for Footwashing and Lord's Supper

I. *Call to Consecration*
    A. Reading of 1 Corinthians 11:23-32
    B. Reading of John 13:1-17 while two to four brothers or sisters wash one another's feet.

II. *Distribution of the Elements*

III. *Receiving the Bread*
    A. Reading of Luke 22:1-19
    B. Prayer for the bread
    C. Reading of 1 Corinthians 10:17
    D. Pronouncement—"The body of Christ broken for you"
    E. Eating the bread

IV. *Receiving the Cup*
    A. Reading of Luke 22:20
    B. Prayer for the juice
    C. Reading of Mark 14:22-25
    D. Pronouncement—"The blood of Christ poured out for you"
    E. Drinking the juice

V. *Time of Reflection Before the Lord*